Thriving Beyond Belief

COURAGEOUS, ROOTED, THRIVING WOMEN

Cheryl Scruggs

I am aware that Cheryl and her husband, Jeff, are extremely successful Biblical Marriage Counselors, but I know Cheryl as a sweet, caring friend and prayer warrior.

I think she is doing the work she was born of God to do, and in her new book, *Thriving Beyond Belief*, Cheryl shares good, sound, and honest counsel. She teaches the truth that she herself has learned the hard way to make it easier for the ones who need her help.

—Kathie Lee Gifford
Emmy Award-Winning former Co-host
New York Times Best-selling Author

My mom has always taught me how to think deeply and has been instrumental in helping me understand myself. She has continuously cultivated a safe space to talk about anything, which has ultimately helped me thrive in motherhood, work, and friendships.

—Lauren Scruggs Kennedy
Influencer, Author of *Still LoLo* and *Your Beautiful Heart*
Co-founder of Stranded

What does it mean to thrive? I mean really thrive, living a vibrant life that is satisfying, balanced, and blesses those around you? Cheryl's easy-to-read, hard-to-put-down new book is practical and relative to women of all ages. Women live in a world that wants to grab our joy and keep us in a perpetual motion of movement that numbs us to what's really going on inside the deepest parts of our soul. Cheryl not only presents the relative issues of very real struggles but also gently pulls us back to the center of things—to what matters most—with practical and sage advice on how to get there. I particularly enjoyed pondering all the "Lost Arts" that our modern culture has lured into near extinction. This book calmed my soul. Well done, my friend!

—Brenda Bogart
Artist
Owner and Founder of Bre Bog Art, LLC

Cheryl's personal stories and how her life has changed from lonely to filled-up, from broken to healed, will inspire and encourage you. Her honesty is refreshing, and her guidance is wise. Are you ready for a heart transplant? This book will be a wise guide for you. I hope you will take the time to linger, sit, ponder, and pray as you locate yourself and move forward to a life of thriving.

—Nancy Houston
Licensed Professional Counselor
Author and Leadership Coach

With the voice of a loving and trustworthy advocate, Cheryl guides us toward a counter-cultural life of thriving that extends beyond circumstance or emotional experience. As I read this life-changing book, I felt both inspired and relieved as I remembered a confidence that is rooted deeper than appearances or outcomes. Read this book with a pen in hand and pass it on to a friend. Whether we've realized it or not, this is a message we are all craving and desperately need.

—Nicole Zasowski
Licensed Marriage and Family Therapist
Author of *What If It's Wonderful?*

Cheryl's voice is both wisdom and encouragement wrapped into one big gift, and she beautifully packed that wisdom and encouragement into these pages. This book reframes what it means to thrive and shows us how to do just that, even when our circumstances make us feel as if we're just surviving. This is truly the everyday woman's guide to thrive in any season of life!

—Jordan Lee Dooley
Best-selling Author of *Own Your Everyday* and *Embrace Your Almost*

I am so glad that you are holding this book right now! As you turn the pages and dig deeper into these chapters, you will find incredible tools for a thriving life. Wherever you are in the stages of life—a mom with toddlers, a lawyer, a teacher, or an artist going through trials and tribulations, wandering in the desert—God will meet you on these pages and equip you to thrive right where you are! Cheryl has a passion to see the hearts of others thrive beyond belief, and her story and journey will equip you for your own journey to thrive in all your stages of life!

—Anne Neilson
Author and Artist
Owner, Anne Neilson Home & Anne Neilson Fine Art

Have you ever wondered why your life doesn't look or feel as abundant as the life Jesus says He came to give us? Let Cheryl show you how you can thrive, even when life offers hurts and challenges that tempt us to doubt God's goodness. What a helpful resource!

—Lysa TerKeurst
#1 *New York Times* Best-selling Author
President, Proverbs 31 Ministries

Cheryl is honest, relatable, and deeply wise. This book made me feel seen. If you've ever struggled with finding peace in the chaos or finding true contentment in your life *as it stands*, this book is for you. As a woman who is constantly striving, this book deeply spoke to and challenged me in ways I didn't even know I needed.

—Kait Tomlin (Warman)
Best-selling Author, Dating Coach
Founder, Heart of Dating

Cheryl walks the talk when it comes to thriving. She models what it looks like to go through the ups and downs of life and still rise above. Her intentionality in thriving emotionally, mentally, spiritually, and physically will inspire you to have a plan to do the same!

—Debra Fileta
Licensed Professional Counselor, Best-selling Author
Founder, Debra Fileta Counselors Network

Reading the heartfelt hope of Cheryl Scruggs words infused my soul with the hope that I don't have to feel worn and weary by the demands of everyday life and challenging relationships. Cheryl formulates the words that often lodge in our throats and helps us find not just our own voices again but also our ability to move beyond the mundane—and our pain—into a life worth living.

—Amber Lia
Best-selling Author of *Food Triggers*

Thriving Beyond Belief

Published by CJ Thrive, LLC

Printed in the USA

Produced with the assistance of Fluency Organization, Inc.
Cover layout and interior design by Inkwell Creative

To my husband, Jeff.
Your deep, heartfelt love, support, compassion,
non-judgmental spirit, forgiveness,
and unconditional acceptance of me is what
helps me thrive in life.
God has brought us
through so much in this life,
and he continues
to walk ahead of us as we continue on
the life journey he has planned.
Words cannot express my commitment,
my loyalty, and my deep and
intimate love for you.
Thank you for loving me well and being
my best friend.
I love you.

ACKNOWLEDGMENTS

IF I TRIED TO WRITE THIS BOOK 25 YEARS AGO, I couldn't have done it. I was 38 years old, and I thought I was courageous, rooted, and thriving! I was definitely more mature and wiser than in my 20s, and God had grown me up and matured me in so many ways, but I had no idea how much more he had planned or how he would continue to mature me until this present day (and will do so until the day I die).

What I have realized in each season of my life is that God continues working his plan in and through me and, more than that, I will never "arrive." He has lots more chiseling, shaping, and molding to do, and this pushes me forward to truly thriving, while being rooted and courageous!

I have so many people to thank. I wish I could name them all and express how they have played a role in my life up until now.

To my daughters, Brittany and Lauren. You allowed me room to learn to parent God's way. Thank you for your gifts of forgiveness and grace, time and time again.

To my lifelong, grace-filled friends. We continuously, without judgement, accept each other fully with grace for our weaknesses and strengths. Thank you for offering me unconditional love, challenge, listening, and encouragement no matter what season, struggle, or exciting thing I have going on. Your friendships are priceless, and I value them more than words can say.

To my special friend, Brenda Bogart, for providing the amazing artwork of her "Jungle Girl" for the cover of the book and for introducing me to Mary Ann Lackland to guide me in this endeavor.

To those who have been cheering me on to get this book out there and who have played significant roles of love, faith, encouragement, wisdom, inspiration, compassion, and hope. I couldn't have done it without you: Jason and Lauren Kennedy, Rod and Paulette (Greene) Roberts, Michael and Debbie Rasa, Bill and Brenda Bogart, Nancy and Ron Houston, Jonathan and Taylor Angelo, Mike and Kim Clinard, David and Elizabeth Sparks, Tracy and Denise Metten, my NLL group, Ben and Ashleigh Pogue, Anne Neilson, Dana Crawford, Sharon Kendall, Rosie Donahue, and my loyal Thriving Beyond Belief podcast listeners!

TABLE OF CONTENTS

CHAPTER ONE

THRIVING IS LIVING

LIFE, MARRIAGE, SINGLENESS, WORK, PARENTING, and relationships can be hard and the struggle is real. But I know women who are learning to thrive in the midst of it all. This book you're holding is an outlier. It frames thriving in a new way. And it paints a different picture of abundant living than what you often hear. I want to make a strong case for why the external stuff we desire and our culture craves—the perfect house, the cars, the ideal marriage, well-behaved kids, and money—ultimately doesn't bring women lasting fulfillment.

And it's okay if you don't believe me even as you read that sentence! I spent a lot of time in my twenties and thirties convincing myself of the same thing, so I get it. We are all trained to think that if we could just get our external stuff fixed or appear better to other people, we would have it all.

And *then* we would finally be happy.

I've come to see life another way. Your ability to live abundantly will always be largely irrelevant of your circumstances. Instead, true thriving is about learning to accept and deal with what's going on inside of you—despite your circumstances. This unique journey of self-discovery is the better way to the better life that we're all seeking.

It sounds counter-cultural because it is. After all, a thriving woman is a paradox. She's learning to deal with reality (the way things are now) *and* live the life she imagines. She's both a realist and an optimist. She's a dreamer, but she's rooted. The closer a thriving woman gets to realizing her life's purpose, the more she understands that true prosperity is nothing like what she once thought it was. It's not perfect circumstances; it's perfect peace within those circumstances. Wanting our outward circumstances to improve is not wrong. Especially if the reason we want that to happen is because we think it will bring peace. The problem comes when we believe financial security, a loving spouse, a better job, happy children and grandchildren—if we only had "that"—then our lives would be on a fast-track to fulfilment.

I understand why women strive for a greater sense of external security. For one thing, it's easier. It is much, much harder to put all that aside, take a long look inside first, and work on yourself. Frankly, people don't want to deal with the pain associated with what they'll discover there. But being self-aware and growing as a person doesn't always have to be painful. Everyone has emotional wounds and regrets from their past. But try summoning the courage to face it and sort through it. Then an interesting thing happens. You'll start seeing how all your external stuff intimately relates to your inside stuff. You'll start to enjoy your external circumstances even more. You'll improve almost every relationship you have. And that's just the beginning of thriving.

My vision is for women to live an abundant life from the inside out in every area and practice the lost arts of being a vibrant human being. I envision women who are energized and enjoying more of what matters most spiritually, emotionally, physically, mentally, and relationally. I want to show women in practical ways how to "be known" to themselves and to others as they really are and learn to be vulnerable. I've seen it happen time after time in my work with women over the years. Real, lasting satisfaction comes from women knowing who they are—and accepting what they discover about themselves. And it starts with knowing who God made them.

That's where I'm coming from, and I'm so thankful you've joined me for this journey. There is a reason why you picked up this book. I'm sure of it. When women can visualize closing the gap between life as they know it—and the life they could be living—they will take action. They want to (and will) thrive when they know how to start. My *Thriving Beyond Belief* podcast and our online community provides what I hope you'll find in these pages: encouragement, support, and strategies to better manage stress, create healthy relationships, and steadily build a life beyond imagination. The people I've interviewed and met with over the years (and others who counsel and encourage me) have taught me so much about a fulfilling life. I share that same sage wisdom in order to help more people thrive more consistently in more areas of their lives.

Sometimes it's a life-altering event or trauma that shakes us out of our mediocrity. At other times, it's another person who challenges us and pushes us to take chances. Into every woman's life comes unexpected moments of deep awareness when we realize our lives are just passing us by and we need to do something about it. Whatever or whoever it is, and whenever it happens, that's your chance to get out of the norm and take courage, flourish, and shine. And I don't want you to miss a single opportunity to do so.

Where are you in Life?

Think back on a time when you were enjoying your relationships more, or exceling in your job, or feeling more connected to your community. What did that feel like? Describe it in your mind and note all the details. Now think about a time when you consistently prioritized your health. What was that like? When was the last time you pursued personal interests like reading or learning something new—just for the pure enjoyment of it? What do you treasure most about those days? If you've ever thrived in any area of your life, you most likely remember something about how great it felt to be alive, free, and finally living on purpose. And my guess is that when you remember, you long to return.

In my experience as a Biblical marriage counselor, author, and podcast host, I've met women from all walks of life. They fall into three general categories. First, there are women who have never known what it is like to live life on purpose. You see them everywhere. They are beat down and exhausted by living. For them, life is just about existing, not truly living. The second category is the largest one. It's the women who have experienced a small taste of abundant living in one area or another—and they want more. They simply don't know how to get there and stay there. These women crave purpose. They recall the pure joy of achieving something that mattered to them, and they want to find their way to that exhilarating feeling again.

The third category is the rare women for whom thriving is living. They have figured out what it takes to get to that next level of living more consistently. And they're willing to put in the hard work to see results. They try to practice self-awareness. They're working on being in true community, fully known for who they are, imperfections and all. For them, life doesn't grow boring or mundane because they never think they've "arrived." Thriving women are lifelong learners for whom the next decade is always better than the last. I know these things are true because I'm living it daily.

Most women I know want some of that. They want to feel more connected, not disconnected. We all desire to gain a better understanding of ourselves and challenge ourselves to live a life of abundance. But we don't know when or where to take the next step. So many women today are putting one foot in front of the other without ever knowing who they are, how they are made, and what they are gifted to do. There is little to no understanding of any of that, which makes it so exciting for me when women finally learn what they need to know.

Life has cycles and seasons. Where are you in life? In what season do you find yourself in? Singleness, marriage, children, the death of a loved one, illness, work, retirement, the empty nest? You may move through these cycles in sequences, or you may skip or repeat some of them. Women experience long seasons when life is painful and shorter seasons when it's relatively stress-free. At any given time, you might be thriving in one area, and not so much in another. And if you're like most women, you probably aren't necessarily always aware when you're not living up to your potential. You may have no clue what you're missing because you think you're locked into your particular situation. It is what it is, so why try to change, right? Self-defeating thoughts like that creep in whenever we exchange thriving for merely surviving and getting through our day.

But life has a way of reminding us in still moments that there must be something more. The choice is ours to make. We can settle, ignoring that quiet call to something bigger and more joyous and more prosperous. Or we can be willing to try new strategies for getting beyond where we find ourselves today. Notice I said be "willing." Willingness to try is all I'm asking for at this point.

WHAT KEEPS US FROM THRIVING

We need to know not only what we can do that leads to thriving, but also what is *not* going to get us there. Take a look at some of the following things that hold us back when we want to go forward. See if any of it sounds familiar.

CONFUSING POTENTIAL WITH PERFECTION

All we're really looking for is progress. My friends know that I like to look up the definitions of words and muse on their meaning. What I like about the word "progress" is that even if all you manage today is take a few small steps in the right direction, at least you're moving forward. Don't be too hard on yourself. It's a journey. Getting farther down the road—even just a little bit—will get you that much closer to where you want to be.

It's so important to understand that slow progress is still progress, especially when you prefer to see instant results. I know. It's hard when you backslide or get stuck trying to make positive strides in an area of your life. The temptation is to give up, throw up your hands and say, "Well, I tried to change but that didn't work. So I quit." Or we go on a major guilt trip because we're not meeting our own expectations we set for ourselves. That's why I want you to realize at the start of this journey that thriving at its essence is about consistency—not perfection.

Think of the people you admire most. I guarantee you they are not "always" on point. How do I know that? Because they are human, just like you and me. If we confuse thriving with perfection, we put too much pressure on ourselves and think, "There's no way I could always do this right. So I don't think I'll even try." If we confuse perfection and progress, we miss the joy of simply learning to live more abundantly, more consistently.

NOT KNOWING WHERE TO START

It's not for me or others to determine what areas of life you want to focus on for your journey. That's the best part. It's your decision, and you get to choose. Life is about deciding where *you* want to thrive today and then making efforts to steadily grow in those areas. Some people would call this part of the process taking action. But I avoid thinking in terms of action plans and steps 1-2-3 to get where you want to go. Thriving, as I see it, is not a punitive thing where if you don't "do these certain steps" you will never get there. I'm looking for a more natural approach to living that works in the real world.

How do you develop areas of your life where you'd like to see some progress? Some people read books to nurture their awareness, for example. But you don't have to necessarily be a book reader. You'll find plenty of suggestions in this book, then you'll have to decide what works best for you and be intentional about what you need to do to grow in one or more areas spiritually, mentally, emotionally, relationally, and physically.

NOT SETTING BOUNDARIES

Sometimes I see someone whose entire life is being directed by someone else's problems. They don't have a chance to thrive. For example, I watch some women give in to inordinate pressure from siblings regarding caring for aging parents. And I think to myself, "This person's not thriving because she's taking on things she shouldn't take on alone." It's something I can spot in someone else's life because I've been there myself. When I went to counseling, I learned that long before I had children of my own, I was already parenting. I now understand the danger in trying to be our parents' parents or parenting our siblings. We instinctively take on a lot that isn't ours to take on alone, and that's a big reason why so many of us are nowhere near living the life we're designed to live.

This is some hard truth, and it took me a long time to realize it about myself. Many years ago I had to realize that I couldn't live my life for the sake of others. Like many people, I used to try to help those I love and "make it better" for them—whatever *that* looked like. I was putting increasing pressure on myself to manage others' happiness, and one day I had to stop. When you are living your life trying to be responsible for others' choices, you condition people to accept that as normal. It's normal for you and it's normal for them. They get used to your doing that. When you stop doing so much, or attempt to stop, they wonder, "What's going on? Why aren't you making everything better for everybody anymore?"

I know I'm not alone in this because I see many older parents trying to dominate their adult children's lives. Those children are facing some difficult decisions. Family can need much more from you than you can give. Ironically, many people who are sandwiched between their parents and their children eventually start doing the very same thing to their sons and daughters. They assert control over what their adult children are doing and the choices they are making—repeating the very thing they resented their own parents for doing.

The longer I live, the more I believe that you must understand "you" first before you'll have a better idea of what needs to adjust in your relationships with others. This is part of the hard work and the whole journey of learning to thrive.

THRIVING, HAPPINESS, AND RESTING IN THE PAIN

I hate to throw this out at such an early point in the book because I'm afraid some of you will stop reading! But here goes: Thriving doesn't necessarily equal happiness.

Hold on. Won't thriving make me *happy*? Isn't that the deal? I'm learning the hard way that this isn't always true and let me explain why. Right now as I'm writing this book, my husband, Jeff, has prostate cancer. I feel as if I'm thriving more than ever in life, but am I happy that he has cancer? Am I happy that we're having to deal with this? And that our life together has changed? No, I'm not happy about any of that. I'm super sad. Do I have a positive outlook? Do I trust God? Do I know God's got this situation, no matter what? Yes.

But ask me if I *feel* happy. No, I don't.

It's okay to *feel* that you're not thriving—every once in a while or even much of the time. You're not always going to be "on" it, you know? You won't always be feeling it on a certain day or during a particular season of life. There is a point when you learn that, in the hardest seasons of living, it's okay just to rest in the pain. There are days when we just can't get it together. You can come to a place where you realize that this too is thriving because you're simply not giving up. And that's enough for today.

I'm no expert, but the edge I've been given in writing this book is that I've been through (and am still going through) extremely difficult seasons of life. I've completed heavy-duty stints of counseling at various points and seasons in order to process these painful experiences. And I am still committed to making the most of the one life I'm given and helping others do the same. It's been my passion for a long, long time. Since I was a teenager, I was keenly aware of when I wasn't thriving or moving to a place of thriving, and now I'm in my sixties. In my twenties I even considered applying to medical school to pursue my fascination with exercise, functional medicine, and optimal health. I tried to learn all I could about how and why the body worked the way it does.

Today I write about thriving and host a podcast, but the ironic thing is that I never initiated deep conversations about the meaning of life with anybody when I was younger. Privately, it was a passion of mine, but because I was the oldest sibling, I learned at an early age not to be a dreamer because I had to be "responsible." That was my full-time focus. I had four siblings and was parentified at the age of three, a term I learned from my counselor. My parents expected me to be responsible, and I complied. I followed the rules and learned to put my own needs second, habits I carried well into adulthood.

From the age of 12, I worked at the golf course my dad owned 35 hours a week in the summers. I didn't think anything of it because I had to do it. But I missed out on sleepovers and regular summer stuff kids do. Then I put myself through college, taking a full load and working two and three jobs at a time. I missed a lot of the true college experience with friends who had a lot more disposable time than my cocktail waitress gig allowed! Looking back, I wonder when I did homework, studied, or slept. I made good grades, so it must have happened somewhere! I was a floundering person as a young adult, making my own way in the world without direction from my parents or any other adult.

While at college, I majored in marketing, I played on the

girls golf team and I had an eating disorder. I worked out compulsively. I became bulimic but had no idea what that word meant. Why I felt compelled to take exercise and eating to an extreme was a mystery to me and a complete secret to others. I see now that my secrecy extended far beyond bulimia. I quickly cultivated an entire life of undisclosed thoughts and feelings. I never complained. Rarely shared intimate emotions. And quietly carried all my dreams for what I wanted to do with my life without telling anyone anything about me. This deeply unhealthy behavior would later destroy my marriage. From the age of 19 to 24 I battled my eating disorder, trying to break the habit completely alone. In fact, when I married Jeff at 23 years old, he did not know I was bulimic. That should tell you a lot. After many years, I finally beat it by sheer willpower. Never went to counseling. Never confided in someone. Never sought professional help.

Not surprisingly, when Jeff and I married, I had no idea how to connect emotionally with another person. Neither of us did. But we were connecting sexually and we were successful at our jobs, and that's all that seemed to matter for a while. We looked like the perfect couple. People actually called us Barbie and Ken. Jeff and I moved to Los Angeles to pursue jobs in sales and marketing, and we were flourishing and really "living the life" in one sense. Yet there was a major flaw in our relationship, and I didn't know how to access a solution for it. A dangerous fault line ran down the middle of our marriage but I had no clue how to fix it. So I did what I always did, following the same pattern of hiding from myself and the truth. I tried to hold my marriage together and do what had been ingrained in me for many years: act responsibly.

Therefore, I didn't tell Jeff how much I was struggling with the lack of emotional availability in our marriage. I wouldn't confide my feelings. I woke up every day just hoping that maybe this was the day we could have a meaningful conversation. We lived like that for years until I did the most irresponsible thing I'd ever done in my life. A heavily compliant person with a fully intact moral compass, I ended up having an affair with someone who worked at the same company I did. Worse yet, I asked my wonderful husband for a divorce. Seven extremely difficult years later, Jeff and I remarried and we're still married today. How that all transpired is a story in itself, and we have shared the details in various settings for many years. We even wrote a book years ago about our experience, and our interview with Dr. James Dobson has played on Focus on the Family's radio program twice a year for many years. So it's natural for me to share stories from my life throughout this book to demonstrate the many seasons in women's lives—the good, bad, and ugly. Because I was so lost in my twenties, I want women to thrive as early as possible and understand what it means to have a rooted and purposeful life from the outset. At the same time, because I'm in my sixties now and thriving more than I ever have, I believe it's never, ever too late.

Everything Jeff and I touched seemed to turn to gold before our divorce. Looking at our lives in our twenties and thirties, would people have thought that my husband and I were thriving? Without a doubt. Even when we struggled, we always landed on our feet. I remember when we encountered problems getting pregnant, we underwent in vitro—a relatively new procedure back then. It worked for us almost immediately and we gave birth to twins. Our doctor even featured our infertility journey and pregnancy in a medical book he was writing. Everything on the surface of our lives went so smoothly: no upsets, no wrinkles. To others it looked convincingly like I knew what I was doing, because women's general definition of success involves a formula of external things. And we had all of that. A house with an ocean view in Palos Verdes. Two adorable girls. More success than we could have dreamed.

But so much was going wrong inside.

I was lonely. My marriage was falling apart and taking my family with it. I was good at my job, but it held no meaning for me. Now I know I have other talents and gifts that fulfill who I am as a person, but no one encouraged me back then to figure out what those were. That's another huge part of thriving—discovering how God has gifted you and where your talents are—and yet it's often ignored. So we show up for jobs we don't even like, day after day, and wonder why we're unhappy.

Just after Jeff and I divorced, something remarkable happened: I became a Christian. I didn't know I wasn't a Christian until I became one! God then began showing me that he wanted me to pursue reconciliation in my marriage... after I had had an affair...after I divorced my wonderful husband...and after I let my precious family fall apart. To say that reconciliation was going to be difficult is an understatement. It didn't just seem difficult; it felt as if it would be impossible.

I had done things I wasn't proud of, and I couldn't imagine picking up the pieces and putting them together. I had no idea how to go about this arduous task. In no way did I feel as if I were thriving at this point in my life. In fact, so many people, good people, were even telling me not to attempt reconciling my marriage.

"Cheryl, don't do it," they told me.

Some actually said, "You *can't* do it."

And there were those who told me straight out, "I doubt God will ever do that for you."

With those words ringing in my head, I was extremely cautious because I didn't know what would (and would not) happen. But at the same time, I remained very curious because God was up to something big, despite the negative feedback I received from some significant people in my life. And that's why I did not quit. I did not give up. For seven years I worked on putting my marriage back together. I was doing some seriously hard work on myself, but also I often just rested in the pain because it took so long to process, undo, and redo all that we'd lost as a family.

Resting in the painful seasons of life is the image God gives in Isaiah 40:31 when he says we can "Rise up with wings like eagles." But sometimes we're doing well if we can just accomplish what the second part of that verse describes: "...they will walk and not faint." Sometimes life is so tough that if we can somehow manage to walk without fainting, we're doing okay. If we can get through our day and not fall apart at the end, that's enough. Sometimes we have to sit and cry for an hour or so before we can get going again. That's also part of being human. It's a natural part of dealing with the heartache that comes from everyday living in this broken world, no matter who you are. Isaiah 40:1-2 describes God comforting us in these moments. It says, "Comfort, oh comfort my people...Speak softly and tenderly to Jerusalem, but also make it very clear that she has served her sentence, that her sin is taken care of—forgiven! She's been punished enough and more than enough, and now it's over and done with." (MSG)

The last thing I want to do in this book is communicate a false message about abundant living that smiles and says, "No matter what you're going through, you've just got to be thriving. You must feel happy, no matter what." I certainly don't feel that way about my own life today. But I used to. I can remember being in my thirties and forties silently urging myself a dozen times a day, "You have to keep it together, Cheryl. You *have* to keep it together." I had to pretend, or so I thought. Meanwhile, things were rapidly falling apart all around me. Rest in the pain? For the longest time, I had no idea what that would even look like.

Now I know that resting in the pain during the hard seasons of life is necessary, and it may look different for different people. Much depends on how difficult the painful season is and how much rest you need. For example, if I'm just having a stressful day, resting means I make time to replenish myself by reading more of a book I'm enjoying. But after I went through one of the most challenging experiences of my life when one of our daughters was seriously injured in an accident and nearly lost her life, I found that I could not concentrate at all, much less read a single page in a book. In fact, I went months without reading and cried more tears than I knew I had in me. However, I see that even then I was thriving—exhausted, but resting in the pain. I'll explain more later how that happened, but for now, I want you to think about what would help you to rest in the painful seasons of life. We must take care during the difficult seasons and not keep pushing ourselves to the limit.

THRIVING STARTS NOW

Women often feel that they can't add one more thing to their already crowded lives—but putting in the work and learning the skills required to get more from life actually sets them free. Here's the thing: it's possible to thrive without having perfect circumstances. You *can* live an amazing life in the most chaotic and sometimes traumatizing situations and circumstances you never thought you were going to have to deal with. You can. And I wrote this book to show you how.

CHAPTER TWO

GETTING FROM HERE TO THERE

FIGURING OUT EXACTLY WHAT WE MUST DO TO transition from life as we know it to the thriving life we want is tough. The idea of getting "from here to there" so we can live abundantly speaks to our world in especially relevant ways today. We're all re-setting what normal life looks like after the pandemic. Perhaps more so than at any other time in our lifetime, the journey from here to whatever's next looks cloudy and uncertain. Deciding to thrive in an uncertain world is scary. Some of you may have even lost sight of "there" and wonder what your future is now and how you can ever reach it. Is it even possible anymore?

I'd like to break it down into manageable steps and challenge you to look at thriving from several different angles:

spiritually, physically, emotionally, relationally, mentally. It's important to me that this book not pressure anyone into making changes in any of these areas. The best motivation is based on how much something means to *you* personally. In other words, I want you to *want* to thrive and choose your own road in some or all of these key areas. Thriving is not a rigid and fixed route to success to be followed... "or else"!

But I admit that that is my tendency as a firstborn child. The benefit of being a firstborn is that I don't have problems with self-discipline and responsibility. The problem with being a firstborn is that I don't have problems with self-discipline and responsibility! If anything, I must be careful not to go on autopilot and follow a legalistic and stringent plan for improvement. Over time, I've been learning to go with the flow instead and let my thriving be more spontaneous and follow its own path.

New Year's resolutions are an example of fixed and rigid plans to get you from here to there that usually end up in failure. Jeff and I always joke about this every January. I don't go to a gym anymore these days because I work out at home. But every January the gym is packed, right? For about two or three weeks, it's hard to find a place to park. Then a few weeks pass and the crowd tapers off before reaching normal capacity again. Most New Year's resolutions fall apart. Why is that? It's a huge frustration point for many women who planned one thing and did another. They wish they hadn't gained 10 pounds, but they did. They wish they hadn't eaten cookies after dinner, but they did. They wish they could stick to a resolution, but they don't.

What is the underlying cause of this disconnect between our intention and reality? Do we need more encouragement?

Is what we set out to do too hard, too soon? We must find out. We don't need to beat ourselves up about it but rather understand ourselves better and give ourselves more grace as we try our wings in new ways of living and doing. It's a good idea to step back and ask yourself, "What is my season of life right now? And what goals are realistic for me *at this time*?" If you have a handle on that, and promise you won't take on too much at once, I believe you're ready to explore the thriving strategies outlined in the rest of this chapter and start setting some achievable goals.

THRIVING SPIRITUALLY

I'd been angry at Jeff for years. He didn't even know it. It felt as if I were up against an immovable brick wall between us all the time, making it impossible for us to connect. As I've said, I started going down this path that led to an emotional and then ultimately physical affair. There were so many devastating choices that led to this spot, but one of the most harmful is that I asked no one for wisdom. I thought I was right. I was never looking for an affair, but my actions were driven by the all-consuming thought, "I can't live like this any longer."

Divorce seemed the only solution until the day I got divorced. In a book Jeff and I wrote together about our marriage, divorce, and remarriage, one of the chapters starts out describing the events of August 21, 1992, as the worst day of my life. That was the day I got divorced. I was at the courthouse thinking the whole time, "What am I doing?" I stood in front of the judge as they granted the divorce and the question pounded inside my head and heart, “What am I doing? I don’t know why I’m doing this. I don’t really want this.” But I felt as if I didn't have anywhere else to turn. I didn't know what more to do. I didn't know how to make it better.

Jeff and I had been going to church in Dallas for over a year prior to the divorce. In the fall after our divorce, I began attending another church. Here, God and the Bible came alive for me. But the experience of a relevant and personal faith was new to me. I never knew I could study the Bible and certainly didn’t understand or know about a personal relationship with Jesus. I wasn't a Christian yet, and I didn't realize that God had been chasing me for quite a while.

At church, I heard a clear message about what Jesus says about living the abundant life. A verse of scripture I return to often is John 10:10. It explains that Jesus came to give us life (meaning capital “L” eternal Life in heaven for eternity)—but even better, he can give us life more abundantly right now. "More abundantly" means having a superabundance of something—a fullness of joy and strength that affects us in our spirit, soul, and body. When I found out that Jesus offers a way of living that is meaningful and completely satisfying, and it was available to anyone, I wanted it. If abundant living was truly an option for me, I decided I would take Jesus up on this offer two months after my divorce was final. I was 33 years old and that decision put me on a journey of knowing who I was as a woman for the first time. What happened next changed everything.

LIFE THROUGH A SPIRITUAL LENS

Many women have never looked at life through a spiritual lens. It's like seeing the world through a pair of special glasses. What I'd like to suggest is that you try some on, take a look at your life, and see if you see anything in a different way. Unless someone is a staunch atheist, most people realize we all have a spiritual component of who we are. For some, it's dormant or it's new to think along these lines. For many, spirituality is something they borrowed from their upbringing—it's never been truly their own. And for others, their faith is everything.

I hadn't realized until I was 33 years old that I didn't even know myself spiritually, emotionally, mentally—none of that. During the first 33 years of my life, I wasn't really living. In the last 30 years, I've come to know what life means. Oh, I had fun before, don't get me wrong. I had tons of friends, I played golf in beautiful places, and Jeff and I traveled. But now I know what it takes to truly live because I began a journey to uncover my purpose for living and to understand God's love. I live in a way today that impacts me spiritually—but also in every area of my life. I'm in my seventh decade of living, and I'm still on that journey. I feel as if I'm learning new stuff all the time about how to develop as a whole person, and it all began with this spiritual component.

My husband teaches men to step back from life and say, "Where's God in all this? Where's my faith, if I truly believe God has a plan for me?" Thriving spiritually doesn't mean life is trouble-free. The other day I listed the spiritual markers in my life thus far. I wouldn't label everything on that list as thriving: an affair, divorce, seven long years waiting to remarry my husband, Lauren's accident, Jeff's cancer. Life has had its difficulties, but I can see me thriving in all of it. Thriving spiritually helps you decide what you're going to do with the realities of life. Paying more attention to who you are spiritually—wherever you are on the maturity spectrum—will help you choose how you're going to react to life's inevitable trials and sorrows.

THRIVING EMOTIONALLY

In my experience with women, I've seen negative emotions and unhappiness slow many people down. Loneliness is a big one. Women of all ages and stages in life sometimes feel lonely. That's life and it's normal. Depending on how extensive that loneliness becomes, however, the ramifications can be catastrophic.

THE BLAME GAME

For me, the loneliness I experienced in the first few years of my marriage was such a big deal. It was one of the reasons why I eventually gravitated toward the unexpected attention I received from another man at work and began a ridiculous relationship. It started by spending hours talking and connecting at a heart level. We developed an emotional relationship that eventually turned physical, but the emotional connection remained the focus. All because I was lonely. I was not looking for an affair. In fact, I never dreamed I could be capable of ever doing something like that.

Negative emotions will keep you from taking a new step toward a thriving life. Stuffing our feelings inside tends to keep us grounded in the past. We must be brave enough to deal with these emotions and realize the unique and powerful ways something as innocent as loneliness affects us.

Learning to thrive doesn't involve abandoning or changing our circumstances, as tempting as that might be. A woman may be single and lonely, for example, but getting married isn't necessarily going to fix her problems or take away her loneliness. Many women will testify that it's possible to be married and still feel lonely. Likewise, married women who are discontent with their lives may think, "In order for me to thrive, I'm going to have to leave my husband. He's holding me back from being happy." I hear that a lot. Or young moms think, "I'm not going to be able to really live until my kids are grown and out of the house." All of these are variations based on a lie. Absolutely.

Because we are often too busy to be introspective, we reflexively point to other people and things as the root cause of our unhappiness. We shine the spotlight on their faults and blame others for our emotional instability. But that only gets us so far. We can only work on changing ourselves, not other people. From my experience, what you *think* is holding you back is most likely not the thing holding you back, especially if you think your dissatisfaction is someone else's fault. The challenge is to go way deeper inside of yourself to find out where and why you're not living a life of abundance and start right there.

The journey begins by asking yourself, "What parts of my misery are about *me*? What pain am I the cause of in my life?" I don't mean assigning blame to yourself and wallowing in guilt. I'm just saying it's essential to truly know who you are and how *you* are impacting the rest of *your* life. Much more on this later—it's that important.

NOT BEING EMOTIONALLY SELF-AWARE

When I say a certain woman is thriving, what do you picture? How she looks? What car she drives? What her adult children do for a living? There is so much focus on the external when we're trying to define what living in abundance really means. We look outwardly to measure if someone is successful, prosperous, and happy. When we do that, we short sell and downplay the greater hidden value of everything that's inside a person. So let me ask you a different question. What kind of person, friend, daughter, mother, or wife are you becoming? The answer to that is really worth something—but it's not talked about as often in the world. Unfortunately, our culture teaches us to put little emphasis on being self-aware. It discourages being open with others about who we are and what we're struggling with.

I'm not sure of all the reasons why that's true, but maybe one reason is because we're all too busy to slow down and look inside ourselves. Another reason our culture doesn't prioritize self-awareness probably has to do with the emotional energy it takes to focus on and develop our character. It doesn't happen overnight. Another reason why we don't do it has to do with the fact that developing character sounds like watching paint dry, right? Boring! Finally, and here is perhaps the biggest reason we avoid becoming more self-aware: it can be scary to take a long look and deal in a healthy way with who we are (and aren't) becoming as a woman. What do we do with what we find?

Take a moment to self-reflect. On a scale from 0-10, how vulnerable do you think you are with your closest inner circle, your spouse if you have one, or your kids if this applies? Do they truly *know* you? Are you willing to be known? Why or why not? Do you sense that they wish you were more vulnerable so they could truly know you?

How do you know if you are emotionally thriving? The key characteristics of emotional maturity that we'll cover throughout this book include:

- Taking responsibility and owning mistakes. People with emotional maturity will try to take steps toward changing negative behavior.
- Showing empathy and willingness to share another's burden and understand them.
- Being unafraid of vulnerability and practicing it wisely.
- Recognizing and accepting your needs. It's okay to vocalize these and understand your feelings.
- Setting healthy boundaries for yourself.

There are many reasons why we don't feel great about our lives at any given point. For example, consider how we deal emotionally with the physical part of ourselves. There are so many women who, from a purely physical standpoint, hate their bodies. You may feel that way. Even some of the most beautiful women struggle and avoid looking in the mirror. Other people have health challenges, and they don't necessarily feel good physically all the time. Thriving over the long term involves being acutely aware of all our emotions, however uncomfortable they may be. You can't skip over this emotional part of who you are as you honestly evaluate and take stock of your relational, mental, spiritual, and physical state. You are beautifully designed in this complex, multi-dimensional manner. It's not by accident, so it's worthwhile to see and evaluate yourself in these various ways.

THRIVING RELATIONALLY

Thriving relationally is complex. It has many levels and working parts. Surprisingly, it has much to do with a simple skill called listening. If I could choose one skill for you to work on in order to see dramatic improvement in your relationships, it would be learning to listen. If you will practice this skill, it will transform your worklife and homelife like nothing else can do. I'll spend some extra time here convincing you of this truth.

LEARNING TO LISTEN

If we don't listen well, we may never learn how to deeply engage with others. I didn't learn much about the skill of listening when I was a kid. In fact, my family interrupted each other regularly in all our daily communication. I remember when Jeff first met my family. He was astonished by how much we cut each other off at the dinner table without a second thought! It was impossible for him to follow what we were saying, but it was totally normal behavior for my family.

I didn't learn to listen well, so now I practice very hard and try to keep my attention on the other person instead of what I want to say about me. We all have a need to talk about ourselves and often hope in many conversations that "we" come up sooner than later! That's why I ask you, are you alert when someone is sharing with you? Can you be quiet when someone is talking and sharing? Considering how conversation took place in my home when I was young, I learned to be a pro at interrupting others. It's been a hard habit for me to break. I've really had to analyze why I do this. Sometimes I'm just excited to share, and sometimes I cut in and blurt out something because I feel insecure and anxious.

What intentions do you have when you talk with someone? When it comes to your listening skills, what bad habits do you think might hurt your conversations? I get concerned about being superficial with people. In other words, looking like you're listening but coming across disinterested and preoccupied. Are we truly interested in listening or just biding time with someone because we "have to" or think we should? There are principles of thriving relationally that tie in deeply with our listening skills, so these are things for us to develop, learn, and concentrate on.

Listening must be a two-way street. When we truly listen, we connect with others in a deeper way. Think about how you feel when you notice someone not fully listening to you. We all mentally check out once in a while. But do you find yourself regularly wanting to disengage with others? Do you want to leave mid-conversation? People can read your body language, even if you're not saying anything. How does your not listening make someone else feel? Whether we realize it or not, we listen with our body and it sometimes tells more than we ever say in words.

One time I was told by people who know me well that I came across as unapproachable in a certain situation. That really surprised me because ninety-nine percent of the time I feel confident in my own skin and am excited in conversation with others. But my friends read my body language and saw I was struggling. And I thought I was the only one who knew that I was nervous and uncomfortable! It was a good reminder that we listen to others with our bodies, not just our ears. How do you want someone to feel while sharing their heart with you? Describe it. What would you need to do to ensure they feel that you heard and paid attention to them? Or does your body betray the fact that you're half-listening with arms crossed, avoiding eye contact, or shifting in your seat as if you want to get out of there?

Two things are going on in any conversation you have. You're outwardly hearing words and inwardly processing what they mean. It's important to be aware of both your internal way of listening as well as how you are outwardly listening with eye contact and body language. In order to have great conversation, you have to understand these two sides of yourself that are operating all the time. If you are fully aware and attentive when listening to others, this one habit will foster more and deeper intimacy in all your relationships. And who doesn't want better relationships when it's a proven fact that they lead to greater happiness and satisfaction in all of life?

HAVING CONVERSATIONS THAT MATTER

I have a confession. I sometimes dread being on the phone. I don't always feel like talking to others in person. And there is a big part of me that never wants to attend another baby shower in my life. Yet I train myself to get past those feelings to seek out rich conversations and connect with people in ways that matter. It's good for me and for others. So, I regularly feed my relationships a diet of intentional connection and conversation that goes below the surface of small talk. The key ideas there are being purposeful and going deep. Meaningful conversation is all but lost today. We text and post regularly, but can we say we're significantly connecting with others when we limit our interaction primarily to quick bursts of social media?

Conversation has changed shape over the past few decades because of technological innovations we didn't have when I was growing up. When I left for college, if you wanted someone to know what and how you were doing, you picked up a phone or paper and a pen. My brother and I were at the same college our first year, so every Sunday afternoon we got together in my dorm room to call our parents. We called collect, and they would call us back because Sunday was the cheapest day of the week. Today hardly anyone writes letters, and people rarely speak on the phone. As a parent and grandparent, I'm happy that technology has evolved to a point where we can be in touch with the people we love as often as we want in other ways. I talk to my girls nearly every day. I see my grandkids on the screen at least once a day in video chat. And although there are limitations, I love video chatting with my daughters and seeing their kids because it adds so much to see faces when we talk.

Intentionality and a focus on deeper conversation applies to all your relationships, even people you don't see that often or are not that close to. Think about the last time you were invited to a women's get-together. How do you respond when attending events with other women? I have a hard time being around a group for long lengths of time. People are sometimes surprised to learn that I'm an introvert at heart. The difference between an introvert and an extrovert comes down to how you recharge emotionally. Introverts can love people and be sociable and outgoing—but they recharge by being alone. Extroverts don't recharge by being alone—they get their energy from being around people. Which one are you? This is what I mean when I say I love women, but women also wear me out! When women get together, they tend to stay on the surface in conversation because so much energy goes into quietly comparing ourselves and protecting ourselves from being vulnerable.

My focus today in social settings is not the same as it was 30 or 40 years ago. Back then, I was anxious about what I was going to wear. After going through my closet, I often bought a new outfit and spent at least an hour getting dressed and putting on my make-up. Then I would drive over, worried about my appearance and hoping I looked okay. Once I arrived I would go into extrovert mode, but my default remained self-conscious throughout the event. At the end of the evening, I would feel exhausted. Today my focus is entirely different.

If I'm invited to event with 15 or 20 other women, I intentionally get in a certain frame of mind before I walk out my door. I think, "What am I going to reflect on during this event? Who am I going to talk to? What kinds of conversations am I going to pursue?" Once I arrive, I might see a woman there I don't know very well, so I make time to get to know her. I practice my listening skills and try to connect with at least one other person at a deeper level. This is all by design. It's not just getting in the car, eating appetizers, and feeling bloated afterward. Instead, I'm aware of the value of this experience and approach it a different way.

You can apply these principles to any social situation. For example, intentional conversation with your best friends is how you become better best friends. If you are a mom, think about the last school event you attended with your child. Did you develop tunnel vision involving your kid and his or her teacher and go home as quickly as possible? Or did you notice others around you? Did you introduce yourself to other parents you did not know? Did you notice the vibe, and if so, what did you learn? This is one way you deepen your sense of community and connection, something we'll talk more about in chapter eight. You take an ordinary event that makes up your everyday life, like a parent-teacher meeting or a birthday lunch, and transform it into something more. I'm constantly looking for anything that helps me pursue more depth in my everyday relationships.

Here's another simple example. Sometimes kids are grumpy. They don't want to get dressed for school. They don't finish their dinner. Sometimes I know you have to just skip the teachable moment, make them get dressed, finish making the lunches, and get out the door. That's part of life. But if you're a grandmother, can you step in and unpack that teachable moment when the mom is busy with other things?

As Momo, my grandmother name my grandkids call me, I can do a lot more to help my daughters than I ever could as Mom. I can ask one of my grandkids, "What's bothering you?" And wait. And wait. Sometimes it feels like the silence lasts for two whole minutes (it's really like 30 seconds), but we're eventually getting somewhere and they will open up to me. I can try to help my daughters by asking questions and saying some constructive things to my grandkids that they wouldn't even listen to if it came from their parents.

Do you see what I'm suggesting here? You can pursue a different level of connection with absolutely anyone. You can focus on a child, or a friend, your spouse, or even a stranger you're sharing space with waiting for a flight. I've learned that people will stay on the surface if you stay on the surface, but they'll also go deep if you take the initiative to guide the conversation that way. For example, one of my daily goals is to learn something from another person, so I've learned to listen more than I talk. I also ask questions when I'm with other people. When I'm listening to someone else's story, I'm always thinking of follow-up questions to drive the conversation to a more meaningful level. For example, I might ask, "Why do you feel that way?" or "What do you think motivated you to do that, go there, try that, say that?"

This section on thriving relationally either excites, bores, or terrifies you. If you're an introvert, your personality may instinctively keep you from engaging others this way. But you can practice it on a smaller scale. You can engage your spouse or your best friend in a more significant way. It didn't come naturally to me when I first started doing this. I didn't grow up this way. Remember, I'm one who didn't have much opportunity or guidance about having serious conversations with anyone about the meaning of life or what was important to me when I was younger. You may have been raised by emotionally disconnected parents in a family that didn't go there. It doesn't matter. If you want to do something to break that chain, do so. I wanted to really know my kids. I didn't do it perfectly—and still don't. But I tried something different than how I was raised. And it worked.

THRIVING PHYSICALLY

There are four aspects of who you are physically. There is the way you see yourself (perceptual). Second, there is the way you *feel* about how you look (affective). This has to do with your emotions, feelings, etc. Third, there is also the thoughts and beliefs you have about your body and what you think others think about you (cognitive). Finally, there are the things you do in relation to how you look (behavioral). Everything we'll talk about in this book about thriving physically relates to having more control over one or more of these aspects. How you "feel" about how you look physically is very important. How I *feel* physically makes all the difference in my life. I have more energy. I *feel* great in my clothes. I *feel* comfortable with myself, and I *feel* confident.

We all have insecuritites about how we look. Bottom line—I'm not going to look 30 when I'm 80, if I live to be that old. And you're not either! But I've made at least three commitments in this area and have experienced positive results. First, I work out regularly. Second, I changed all my personal care products like shampoo, moisturizers, and soap to toxin-free, clean products. Third, I am committed to clean eating. Let's start with exercise.

EXERCISE AND THRIVING

Exercise is something I enjoy, but I've also taken it too far in the past. In my case—and this is weird, fair warning—I have to make myself take time off from my workout schedule. Some people work out religiously; I used to work out ridiculously. I have better control over that impulse now. But I have craved exercise my whole life primarily because it's a peacemaking strategy for me. It makes me *feel* calm about myself and all that I have going on. Chemicals and endorphins are real! I like the *feeling* of serotonin flowing through my body and keeping me on an even keel emotionally. (See how these areas begin to overlap?) Exercising is a stress releaser to settle down, get things off my mind, and burn off excess emotional energy like a plane dumping extra fuel. My average is 30 minutes a day, or sometimes I'll take a 60-minute walk. I have a Peloton stationary bicycle at home and at times, like yesterday, I limit myself to only a 15-minute high intensity interval training (HIIT) ride. That was my workout, and I had to be satisfied with that. I generally work out five days a week and that is plenty!

I've never fallen off the wagon. In fact, the only time that I took extended time off from working out was forced. It happened when Lauren had her accident and began her intense recovery. On a practical level, I couldn't schedule workouts because we were all-hands-on-deck during that time as a family. I also had to come to grips with the fact that for the first time in my life, I didn't even want to pour myself into my workouts. Exercise wasn't important at that time. The realization was jarring because exercise was something I had done my whole life! It was still super vital for my mental and physical health, but something unforeseen had happened and I just couldn't do it.

Do you realize how much your emotional and mental wellbeing affects your physical wellbeing? Let me tie this together for you. If you exercise, why do you do it? Do you enjoy exercise? Why or why not? Next, take food. Do you have a healthy relationship with food? And now consider body image—that is physical, but it stems from our emotional state. How do you *feel* about your body image? I once asked a group of beautiful, fit young women why they work out. They were eager to tell me how they worked out, what exercises they did, and where they like to go. But *why* they worked out? They weren't ready with an answer for that one. It's a good question to ask ourselves. A devil's advocate might suggest that our bodies are disintegrating as we age, so why try?

At 63, I'm in the best shape I've ever been in, but I don't look like I did when I was in my twenties. Case in point. One of our best friends is a dermatologist, and he's always saying to me, "Cheryl, I can fix those lips." I'm not against getting some work done, but at the same time I'm opposed to the overuse of it. I once ran into someone that I hadn't seen in 20 years. She recognized me, but I had no idea who she was. That's how much she had changed her outward appearance. Why do you want to look good? Jeff jokes and says that women dress up for other women. He's right! But why do we want to stay healthy? We have to find a motivation that works for us. These are the pertinent questions for you to consider as you tackle the big animal of thriving physically.

CLEAN PRODUCTS

The second significant change I made is something I recommend to everyone. I transitioned into a clean-living lifestyle that increased my energy levels and boosted my overall health. The quality of our physical health primarily stems from the food we eat and the products we use regarding our bodies, including skincare, beauty products, even the household cleaners we use on a regular basis.

Let's consider the product-side of a clean-living lifestyle first. We spend so much time at our homes, raising family, working, and relaxing. So we must pay more attention to what we regularly bring into our home and expose ourselves to. The skin is the largest organ, so it matters what it comes into contact with on a regular basis. This includes things like the lotions and personal care products you use, the make-up you wear, and the cleansers and scents you expose yourself to throughout your home. Do you know exactly what is in those products? Are you aware of potential toxins and harmful chemicals that might be taking a toll on your health and preventing you from thriving physically?

I didn't overhaul the products I use on my skin and in my home all at once. It took time, and I had to research and find substitutes that still got the job done and worked for me personally. You'll have to do the same thing for yourself. Do your research. Discover what works for you. You don't need to break the bank—take it slowly and exchange products one at a time with a safe, healthy, toxin-free alternative. See how you and the other members of your family feel as you transition your home to a cleaner environment. Do your headaches disappear? Is asthma still an issue? Do mysterious rashes resolve once you stop using toxin-laden detergents and soaps?

CLEAN EATING

The third commitment I've made is eating clean. Nobody was talking about "eating clean" in the 70s when I grew up. Our parents did what other parents did: they put food on the table and we ate it! However, I was the only one of my friends who planted a garden behind our house in junior high and tended to my vegetables after school. Way before it was cool or trendy, I was into researching healthy, whole foods at the local library.

What I've learned about myself is to accept that God made me that way for a reason. Becoming an adult activated into super-drive what I'd wanted to do since I was young—enhance every aspect of my life, including my physical health. When I had kids, I prepared meals based on whole foods, not processed or refined items like white rice and pastas with all the nutrition artificially removed. I learned to shop the outside of grocery store aisles where the fresh produce and meat is, steering clear of the middle aisles where most of the processed food is shelved. Jeff grilled wild-caught fish for us, and I made salads with homemade dressings. Reading labels became second nature to me because I wanted to know what was in the food I served my family.

Jeff and I have followed a holistic lifestyle of clean living for so many years. I buy everything organic, including wild-caught seafood along with some grass-fed beef. Jeff and I choose to eat gluten-free, even though we are not gluten intolerant, because we feel better avoiding gluten in our food. We also skip dairy products and prefer milk substitutes like almond milk. I make my own almond milk with my almond milk maker called the Almond Cow—super easy and worth it. Plus, it saves me money!

I've learned many tips from my daughter Lauren who wrote a 90-day guided series about clean living called *The Clean Sweep*. She makes it easy and fun for people to transition into a healthier lifestyle. Lauren writes about ways to help our microbiome thrive by supporting it through the products we use and the food we eat. The microbiome is the colony of bacteria that lives in your brain, mouth, gut, lungs, and skin. It is responsible for protecting against disease and regulating your immune system, digestion, mental health, quality of sleep, and energy levels. The second system she advocates protecting and supporting with toxin-free products and clean food is the endocrine system, a sequence of glands that produce and secrete hormones to support many bodily functions, including sleep, breathing, mood, metabolism, growth, sexual function, fertility, movement, recovery, and more.

So many people are curious about this lifestyle but they think clean eating is complicated—so complicated, in fact, that they are unwilling to give it a try. And there are those who eat chicken strips and consider them moderately healthy because, hey, it's chicken. Some women just get used to brain fog and assume that's just life. There is another, better way. Lauren calls it finding the sweet spot where you are balanced in your approach to food without being so fanatic and rigid that you can't enjoy life.

I'll admit that clean living is a challenge at first because you must declutter your home of unhealthy foods (food with no nutritional value) and get rid of toxic products. You also need to educate yourself and commit to implementing what you learn for the rest of your life. Not just a week or two. This lifestyle couldn't be easier once you get the hang of it. For example, the only spices you really need are pepper and Himalayan salt or sea salt (instead of iodized table salt). On average, it takes me only about 20 minutes to cook a healthy dinner full of natural vitamins and nutrition. That's all. We've even had friends come over for dinner to learn how to cook a clean eating meal, start to finish. Each time, they're amazed at how easy (and delicious) it is.

You won't believe the difference in terms of overall health, greater stamina, clear-thinking, better mood, quality sleep, and sustained energy throughout your day. Once you start to reap the benefits of getting what your body needs from natural foods and healthy products, you'll never go back because you'll be thriving physically—perhaps for the first time in your life.

THRIVING MENTALLY

As women, what we have going on *outside* differs wildly. We're single, married, empty nesters, new moms. We're old, we're young, and somewhere between. I like a little Amos Lee playing in the background, and your playlist may look entirely different. But what we quietly think about *inside* our heads is much the same as women, and as people in general.

Things like, "*What is the meaning of life? Is this all there is? Where do I fit it? Who will love me?*" Some of us are so bewildered by these questions. We're even at a point where we no longer want to think about them. It's emotionally and spiritually painful to come up empty, so we turn up the noise and busy ourselves so that we don't and won't think at all.

PRIORITIZING TIME TO THINK

When is the last time you prioritized structuring your life around pockets and snatches of time when you could just sit and think? That can happen, you know. And it can happen in a lot of different ways. We must be intentional about it, however. Eight hours of sleeping leaves 16 hours in a day. And I can't find 30 minutes to sit and think? Making silence and thinking a priority will take sacrifice. When I was separated from my husband, I got up at 5:00 each morning to journal and study my Bible. With two little girls to raise, I was tired. But regular moments of silence proved vital to my daily survival. Thirty years later, I'm no longer raising little children but I'm still studying and journaling.

Mentally thriving involves being curious about your passions and interests and becoming a lifelong learner in a variety of areas. Easily said by a person whose primary strength is learning, I know. But let me stimulate your thinking. You can read books, listen to podcasts, and go to talks about your side interests like cooking, painting, decorating, sports, or gardening. Like birds? Download a bird-identifier app. Like history? Attend a workshop by a local history professor. Listen to music—and read the bios of the artists you enjoy. Have you ever watched a show called

The Chef's Table on Netflix? Each episode features the back story of how someone became a chef. I love hearing how others find their passion.

People are bored in life because they're not curious and they're stuck in a rut. Using our brains and working our mind are essential activities to staving off mental decline. At the end of your life, what interests will you wish you had pursued? Keep that list short.

Setting aside time for more thinking more often can also challenge you, even to the point of being uncomfortable. People are generally afraid of challenges. They're afraid to prod themselves to think. I've had more than one conversation with couples and women about self-discovery, only to see a deer-in-the-headlights response. When I throw out basic questions about their purpose and intention in living, they look blank. Nothing registers! They've literally never thought about their personal mission in life or what drives them. The alarm clock goes off in the morning and they're busy until they lie down in bed again that night, only to repeat the process the next day.

If you're married, don't be that couple running ragged. If you're single, don't be the woman who only scratches the surface of life. Be different. Think your way into a new kind of living that excites you and drives you every day to improve yourself. Be at your best, learn something new, and challenge yourself mentally.

WHERE YOU REALLY, REALLY WANT TO BE

Let me remind you that a thriving person is not perfect; they are simply consistent in some important areas. They can put into words how and where they want to thrive and explain what that looks like. If you have a good grasp on how you want to thrive, especially when you're young, you make better decisions. Putting in the time to consider what you really want out of life will determine some of the most important decisions you'll ever make. When you're young, you make vital choices about the friends you make, the job you want, the person you choose to marry, etc. But it's never too late to make better choices and more meaningful decisions. You can't undo the past, but you can move forward from it toward a different future.

What is your greatest, wildest dream for your life? In this exercise, before you turn another page, I want you to think about where you are now and how you want to thrive in the future in the vital areas of your life we explored in this chapter. Think about how you're going to get from here to there. Consider where you are spiritually, physically, emotionally, mentally, relationally—the whole thing. What is it that you *most* want from life in these areas? Put words to it.

Do you want to have richer, more satisfying relationships?

Do you want a more intimate marriage?

Do you want to enjoy and maintain better health?

Do you want to grow spiritually? Do you want to explore what that means, if you've never considered the spiritual part of yourself?

Do you want God/Jesus to lead you in your life?

Do you want to learn how to think more deeply and access more of your brain and your thoughts?

Do you want to grow into a deeply intimate person and share yourself with others in a healthy, vulnerable way?

Do you want to learn to understand others better and learn to love at a deeper level?

Do you want to discover your life's purpose and live out of that purpose more consistently?

Now for the bigger, more practical, question. How are you going to get there? If you have no idea, that's normal. I had no idea how I was going to host a podcast in my sixties. I just knew that if I put in the work, something would happen that was beyond my wildest dreams. And it has. I had no idea how I was going to restore my marriage after I was divorced. I just knew that if I put in the work, something would happen that was beyond my wildest dreams. And it has!

There are so many other examples I could point to in my own life and in the lives of others. Now, it's your turn to have a story of your own. Start by completing this sentence and repeat this exercise for every area of life we discussed in this chapter:

I have no idea how I am going to:

____

[your dream goes here]

I just know that if I put in the work, something will happen that is beyond my wildest dreams!

Hold on tight to that thought. It's the first step in a journey that could change your life forever. It's alright that you don't yet know exactly *how* that dream is going to come about. For now, I just want you to keep sketching details of what thriving looks like for you. That's key because people tend to get paralyzed and never take the first step toward their dreams when they can't see exactly where the road ahead leads. We have to get past that insecurity by focusing and re-focusing on a dream that is vivid enough in our minds to motivate us toward small steps of faith, instead of being too afraid to change.

CHAPTER THREE

RECOVERING THE LOST ARTS OF BEING HUMAN

I'VE ALWAYS BEEN A GARDENER AT HEART. THE pandemic gave me extra time to pour myself into gardening at home and creating an outdoor place of calm and peace where I could nurture my plants, think, and be quiet. For many years I've collected books about gardening and can quickly lose myself in a nursery full of plants and flowers. While many nurseries in Texas sell the same things to everyone, like the ubiquitous pansies and decorative kale, I'm a little rebellious. I just can't do what everyone else does.

So I order online from a nursery overseas in Holland, dabbling with new kinds of roses or other rare plants to try. No matter what varieties I bring to my garden, the flowers all start the same way: as a bud. A bud is not a big deal, is it?

It's not colorful. It's small. And if it's a new plant, it's not that obvious what the flower is even going to look like when the bud opens up. But the potential for something spectacular is all there, tightly wrapped up inside that tiny bud. And I get excited about that.

One day it hit me that people are so much like buds in a flower garden. A budding person is not yet all that they are going to be. But the potential is there. Thriving is about unfolding different areas of your life day by day like petals opening on a flower bud, knowing that it takes time to evolve and change into something you can't see right now. Best of all, you don't have to do it perfectly, only more consistently, in order to thrive. Developing your potential, not reaching perfection, is the focus of this chapter.

Maybe you can relate to the imagery of a bud because you're new to this idea of thriving. You're not completely sure what your life, your job, or your relationships are going to look like in the future. But you are willing to work on it step by step. Like a healthy garden, we're all budding in different ways all the time. Some of us are going back to school to get more education. Some of us are moms of young children, teenagers, or college-age kids. Some are newlyweds. And some of us are working on achieving 40 years of marriage to the same person. Whenever and wherever we see growth, it means we're evolving into the kind of woman we want to be one day, even though we're not there yet. Just know that inside of you is everything you need to get there—to blossom and bloom into a whole new way of living. You can thrive spiritually and emotionally, strengthen your relationships, develop community, be more confident in your physical appearance, and deepen your character. I know that is true because I'm doing it, and I've worked with many women over the years who are doing it also. In this chapter are some practical steps you can take to gain momentum—all from a source you might not expect.

GETTING IN TOUCH WITH WHO YOU'RE MEANT TO BE

I recently bought a coffee table book about how to grow vintage roses. Also called old garden roses or antique roses, these varieties were popular prior to the 1860s. Growing roses is tricky. You'd think anyone could do it, but it's not true. They're prone to disease and require a lot of extra attention. The book went back in time, exploring the wisdom and advice of sage gardeners from over 100 years ago. These hints and tips about the way people used to garden in the "old time" describe the lost art of caring for these notoriously high-maintenance plants. The advice may have come from a bygone age before my grandparents were even born, but it is as relevant today as ever. And the pictures! Like so many people whose online reviews I read, I fell in love with the sketches and daydreamed about growing vibrant, healthy roses outside my window that would look just like them.

Honestly, I kept the book for the pictures. And because it made me think. We've advanced tremendously in society, but we have also lost touch with so much along the way. My eyes rested on a phrase in this book that described a certain variety of roses as "the best of its kind, representing the high quality of a past time." It made me think about the lifestyle of those who were growing those roses generations ago. They knew firsthand about a high quality of a past time. They valued priorities like neighbors taking care of neighbors and taking time to rest instead of going full steam all week. (Remember Sunday naps?) It makes me sad to see how our modern culture has lost sight of key practices and priorities from the past because we chose not to continue them in our busy schedules. We forgot. We lost touch. And in my opinion we became less human as a result. It took a book on vintage roses to remind me that we could recapture some of it once again and re-learn what we need to know so we can thrive.

You can't just do "whatever" here and there and end up with beautiful vintage roses like the ones in the book. (I wish!). There are specific growth instructions and planting guides that must be followed to get certain results. So what would happen if we resurrected and absorbed old-fashioned principles and practices about quality living from our grandparents' time into our sometimes hollow lifestyle today? What might change about us? What could be improved? The more I thought about what we've lost in the generation since I was young, the more questions I had. As old-fashioned as it may sound to modern ears, I wonder:

What happened to sending hand-written (with a stamp and everything) thank you notes?

What happened to having meaningful conversations on long walks with our loved ones?

What happened to making regular time in our week just to sit on the porch and do nothing but think deeply about life?

What happened to families playing together and observing family traditions?

What happened to preparing and sharing meals at home with family and friends?

The thing about lost arts and traditions like these is that they had to be present at one time in order for them to be "lost." If we humans had it once, we can find it again. Think about it. What we consider lost arts today were once everyday living for people in another era—but somewhere along the way we got disconnected, and we've been missing out on their value and contribution ever since.

Think about the twenty-somethings and thirty-somethings you know. It's disheartening to me how few regularly seek wisdom from older people. Their community group is typically all the same age, in similar circumstances. In other words, they're gaining wisdom exclusively from their peers! Granted, there are some wise-beyond-their-years kids (I call them kids)—but what about making a conscious connection to older and wiser generations? Why not seek them out and see what they have to say about life and living? I'm emphasizing the importance of in-person communication with that older generation because it takes more effort. As a teenager, young adult, and newly married, I sought my parents' advice, especially my dad. They'd been around the block a few times, had experienced some hard knocks, and knew more than I did.

Your grandparents probably did more of this than your generation does, but when people were sick someone would just go to the hospital just to "sit" with them. Ladies used to visit friends in the hospital and end up sitting quietly for hours. Just to sit there so the ill wouldn't be alone. People rarely do that anymore, but it's worth noting that people felt compelled to be near in order to be a good neighbor, to be a good friend. They may not have had the time, but they *made* the time. They went beyond themselves to figure out what someone needed, and then they followed through.

We don't often "sit with" people today, but the principle still rings true. If we are to embed in our souls the tried-and-true wisdom behind the practices of a long-ago age, we must find ways to follow it in our everyday lives. It's about digging deep into the bedrock of who we are and turning over the soil again and again until we are living in a whole different way. Until we care deeply again. Until we're raising our families differently. Until we're timing our schedules differently. Until we're nurturing our souls in a way that's different than the rest of the world, like a vintage gardener tending the rarest of roses. Until we're thriving.

THE LOST ARTS OF BEING HUMAN

I made a list of what I've been doing over the past 30 years that has enabled me to thrive personally and build a focus around helping others thrive. I call these vintage practices that lead to thriving "The Lost Arts of Being Human" because we've disconnected ourselves from so many habits and priorities of our unique humanness. Our default busy mode setting in the 21st Century makes us feel as if we have no time to do more than we're already doing. How are we going to work in anything new to help us thrive when we sense we are barely hanging on to the basics day to day? Do you see how that limiting mindset takes away from your humanity, reducing you to what some people call a "human doing" versus a "human being"? Humans were designed to enjoy life, not endure it as we frantically complete our to-do lists.

Our goal here is something I've been speaking and writing about for many years: becoming fully and wonderfully human and thriving the way God wants us to thrive. We are created as multi-dimensional beings with facets of our personalities and minds that largely go untapped in a modern age. Each one of us has the potential to think deeply, rest, enjoy life, be virtuous, develop character, become generous and grateful, savor the moment, and be fully alive. These Lost Arts may be simple, but they're potent, powerful principles that make us slow down to take stock of what matters. They also make us brave and willing to try new things, believing we have the potential to move to the next level of the person we're meant to become.

The things on my list are all very simple. Nothing is earth-shattering or revelatory. There are many, many more Lost Arts out there, and I'm sure you'll have your own ideas, too. Here is my running list of what I know has worked for me and many other women who practice these same Lost Arts:

The Lost Art of Thinking

The Lost Art of Resting

The Lost Art of Reading to Learn

The Lost Art of Writing

The Lost Art of Paying Attention

The Lost Art of Conversation

The Lost Art of Phone Calls

The Lost Art of Gratitude

The Lost Art of Savoring the Moment

The Lost Art of Play and Laughter

The Lost Art of Sharing Meals

The Lost Art of Being at Home

The Lost Art of Courage

Making time to think deeply is a foundational Lost Art of Being Human, and it is truly missing in our culture today. So I want to explain it here as a leading example of how these Lost Arts connect us with the vitality associated with an age gone by.

MAKING TIME TO THINK

In our modern lifestyle, we could all benefit from having more down time to stop and ponder life. I call it the Lost Art of Thinking. As pointed out in chapter two, we're not entirely comfortable with the idea of silence and thinking, so instead we regularly sabotage potential opportunities to be quiet and meditate. For example, consider how we routinely fill any hint of silence with noise throughout our day. The radio is on in the car from the moment we start the engine, and we're powering through an audiobook or listening to music and news until we park the car and get out. Tucking in our ear buds, we head out on evening walks, ignoring who and what's around us. Modern society resists silence at every turn. Try to think of a café or restaurant that *doesn't* play soundtracks while you dine. Noise and input are pervasive. Television accompanies us everywhere from airport gates to the dentist's chair! We're even treated to marketing commercials blaring from the gas pump speaker at some stations.

If you're like me, you probably wonder what you would do if you had more silence in your life. One activity you could try is journaling. Journaling is a way to actively capture your thoughts and emotions and process them in a disciplined way. Many years ago, some girlfriends encouraged me to start journaling. Honestly, at that time I thought journaling was so-so. I wondered what on earth I would write about. But upon their advice, I bought a new journal and began writing. At first, I wasn't sure what to do, so I wrote out prayers or jotted some feelings I was having. As time went by, I started thinking of journaling as my chance to record personal conversations with God on paper.

Today, I use journaling in many ways, including as a prayer journal and a processing tool. Sometimes I write about negative thoughts in my journal. But not always. I can also journal about why I'm feeling particularly peaceful or joyful and trace back the positive habits I'm following lately that are contributing to my personal sense of satisfaction. Through journaling, I have learned that I feel calm and at peace when I set some boundaries, for example. I can write about how a hard conversation I had to have with someone actually ended up going okay and how happy that made me.

Cultivating the practice of silence and pursuing the Lost Art of Thinking is like swimming upstream in a noisy and busy world, but it leads to so many benefits. I've cycled through seasons in life when I was journaling often and also times when I was not. Some days I have so much to pen and other days only a few words. But I'm the first to testify to what the habit has done for me—and how it has led to my thriving during some of the most difficult periods of my life. For example, silence makes us more likely to hear from someone other than ourselves. Mentally, we give ourselves a break in silence and stop the self-talk (that's usually negative). We can also refocus spiritually in silence. I've never heard God speak in an audible voice, but I have felt as if his Spirit is giving me some insights and direction that I can't take credit for having come up with myself. I call these sacred times "downloads," and this usually happen when I'm journaling. Some thought or affirmation pops into my head that rings true, and I end up writing about it in silence.

Emotionally, silence encourages me to do a mind-dump on the page and forces me to deal with whatever I'm feeling in a healthy manner. Physically-speaking, this practice of unpacking your thinking has the potential to heal your mind and your body. It gets the anxiety and stress out of your mind and body and onto the paper. Science has shown us the limitations of the human body. Our bodies reach pinnacles of stress. Releasing anxiety doesn't have to involve journaling. The same thing can be accomplished by a walk in the sunshine, the practice of yoga, and other activities that cause you to take a break, reorganize your thoughts, and experience silence. I focus on what I was thinking about while on a walk or during a visit to a favorite shop. Sometimes I do my best thinking spending a Saturday afternoon with Jeff listening to Van Morrison and sipping a glass of wine. At the end of this chapter, you'll get a chance to do the same thing and learn some practical ways to practice the Lost Art of Thinking.

A THRIVING YOU

All the Lost Arts are about thriving. Thriving looks different in everyone's life. Thriving for me is not the same as what it might look like in your unique situation. That's the beauty of it—we are God-designed with a plan and purpose just for us. In this exercise, consider what it would look like for you to thrive in your everyday life. Use your imagination and spend some time journaling and/or reflecting on the following:

Who are you surrounding yourself with when you're thriving?

What are you doing when you're thriving?

When are you thriving the most—how old are you? What season of life are you in?

Why are you thriving then? What's working in your favor?

Where are you in your career, marriage, relationships, etc. when you're thriving at that age/in that season?

What is different about you then? What is the same?

As you move through this book, you'll become more aware of how the Lost Arts of Being Human will challenge your fear of getting out of your norm and taking new chances. What are some dreams you'd like to pursue? Start small. For example, some women would really enjoy taking gourmet cooking classes. Some would like to learn a new language. At some part of every day, the thought crosses their mind, "I wish I could_____________" but they never pursue whatever goes in that blank. Almost immediately, they think, "Oh well, this is just my life. I'll never change it."

If you are one who is settling for "Oh well, this is just my life..." you're missing out. I'm giving you permission to paint the picture of whatever your life looks like if you're thriving—and spend some time with those details in your mind. The more you can visualize yourself thriving and living an abundant and rich life, the greater your likelihood will be to do it.

I hear you now. You're so busy—and you don't have time to incorporate any of these into your life. I know. Have you ever wondered why we don't put more effort into what we *say* means the most to us? For example, married people often tell themselves that once the kids are grown and out of the house they can work on their marriage. Even happily married people say that. But you can have an extraordinary marriage right now—you don't have to wait.

By the same token, I see many single adults putting off the enjoyment of life until they finally meet someone. But they are isolating themselves, unwilling to sacrifice much in the way of meeting quality potential partners. Swiping right or left on a dating app doesn't take a lot of effort and it's low- to no-risk. What is required to find a potential mate with whom we can share the rest of our lives? That's worth paying a price to find out. But it requires taking a chance.

Here's another practical example. Let's say you liked to paint when you were younger. You hear there is a new evening art class downtown, but you hesitate to sign up and the excuses start piling up. You don't know where to park. You're not sure what it costs. "Gosh, your life's so busy right now," some voice warily reminds you. Still, the idea of taking an art class keeps coming up in your heart and mind. So, the question would be: Why not now? Why not give it a try? Yes, there will be a price to pay—your time, your wallet, and even your self-confidence until you get to know more people in the class. But do it anyway!

There is always a fear factor of following through on what we *say* we want our lives to be. I think there's a fear of recovering these Lost Arts of Being Human because of what might have to change in our daily life. Sometimes we're just not down for that. What might you learn? What might you be convicted of? What will your family and friends think if you change your life? Sometimes we even wonder, "What is going to be taken away from me if I try to hear what God wants me to do?"

Sacrifice and change are not naturally high priorities for most people. I can hear it now: "If I go sit in a hospital with somebody for an hour, I'll be behind the whole day." That could be true. But would you really be behind—or would you have moved ahead several steps in your understanding of what's more important in life? I sometimes catch myself bemoaning how much time it will take to go out to lunch with someone during a busy season of life. "That's going to be two hours out of my day. I don't know if I want to do that..." I tell myself. It's not just getting behind schedule that we dread. It's the draining feeling we might experience afterward. Spending extra time with someone who needs us can leave us feeling depleted. It's not always life-giving—even with people we enjoy. Here's the question worth answering. If your presence means so much to someone else, are you willing to pay that price even when you don't feel like it? How will that kind of commitment change you?

WILLING TO PAY A PRICE

What we're fighting against is the natural shallowness in all our lives. It's like gravity weighing us down. You may not be aware that the possibility of a higher purpose could be hidden in each day's most boring routines, like the carpool line and grocery run. Or you may not be convinced that there is much more available if we connect to the abundant life Jesus talks about. Either way, that's what these Lost Arts of Being Human will help you do.

Are we rushing around so much that we can't even follow the next level of life that God's trying to show us? Sometimes, especially in our culture, we want immediate results with as little effort as possible. Yet quality relationships are a time-consuming journey. Parenting, marriage—it's all an enduring journey. Learning to thrive is a long-term journey, but practicing whatever it takes to get there (and being willing to pay the price) will lead you to places that you would not trade for the world.

PRACTICING THE LOST ARTS OF BEING HUMAN

I'll get you started in this chapter with some specific Lost Arts to begin practicing right away so you can build momentum and see results in your personal life and relationships. Each chapter in the rest of the book will conclude with a handful of other Lost Arts to help you connect with your live-giving humanness again and kickstart your ability to thrive.

THE LOST ART OF RESTING

Think about "resting" as "re-setting." You know when you lose power at home and you must reset the digital clock on your oven to the proper date, time, and hour? That's what resting is. Sometimes you've blown a circuit and you need to rest and re-set to function again. Resting is a Lost Art today because we've narrowed the focus to just physically resting, although it can include that. A functional definition of resting is much broader and includes whatever contributes to your mental, emotional, and spiritual calm. It likely involves solitude. Tranquil moments of rest will refresh and restore you as you grow quiet and still in your spirit.

For me, resting is not about taking a nap. I generally don't take naps. But I do try to take time to rest, even for a few minutes, every day. I think of resting in 15- to 30-minute windows whenever I can carve out some time in my day. Let me give you some examples of the variety of things resting can be. It could mean going outside to nurture my plants in the backyard, checking to see what's blooming (and what's not). Just investing those few minutes connecting with nature, being outdoors, and thinking of nothing gives me the mental break I need. It rejuvenates my mind. Sometimes I take a walk outside to rest. Sometimes I listen to a favorite podcast at the end of the day. While I'm cooking, I listen to music and quietly process whatever I've been thinking about all day. Or I may meet a friend for a leisurely meal at a restaurant. All these practices mentally and emotionally de-stress me.

What does resting uniquely look like for you? First, you must give yourself permission to rest and not feel guilty about it. Tell yourself it is okay to take a break and stop doing whatever "you must get done" and re-set for a few minutes. If you don't know where to start, you might schedule a long overdue coffee with a good friend. Sit outside if the weather permits. Feel the breeze on your face and sunshine on your skin. Stay longer than you anticipated. Take cat naps on weekends or go to bed earlier. Sometimes a day of resting looks surprisingly like, "You know what? I'm going to read for two hours today. I'm going to put my to-do list away and do nothing." Young moms say, "Hold on—I've got kids at home. How am I going to do that?" That may be true in your situation. But all of us can find pockets of time just to unplug, let our brain think, and become more aware of how we're feeling inside. Think of these pockets as places that provide mental, emotional, and spiritual shelter.

The reason this habit is essential to thriving is sometimes we are not self-aware enough to know when we *need* to rest. Take stock right now of how you feel. Some symptoms of your need to rest may include: anxiety, a racing mind, jumbled thoughts, brain fog, and feeling overloaded. I've noticed that highly driven personalities find it difficult to rest. They feel guilty when they relax. Some women get anxious just thinking of taking time out to rest. I know this was true of me in my twenties, thirties, and forties when I couldn't see resting as *that* important. Why did I need to rest? When I came to understand that rest could be purposeful—and not wasteful—I felt better about trying to practice it. I quickly became convinced of the benefits of resting and recharging my introvert batteries. Now, I treasure this habit and work it into some part of my day, every day.

Questions to ask about resting:

What are some ways you can mentally de-stress and rest your mind? What are some ways you can emotionally rest? What does "spiritually resting" mean to you?

If you don't know the answer to these questions, what might it look like if you tried to rest mentally, emotionally, and/or spiritually? Think creatively.

THE LOST ART OF THINKING

By now you may be convinced how good it is for us spiritually and emotionally to regularly enjoy periods of silence—with no artificial input. Noise breeds avoidance, while silence breeds thinking. It is the perfect environment to grow still where we empty our minds of any conscious thoughts. Beware, however, that thinking usually leads to deeper thinking. Most people keep their minds focused strictly on the surface of life—deliberately occupying their minds with their to-do lists, the weather, kids' schedules, etc.

It's so much easier to deal with the shallow end, isn't it? It's why some parents talk only about their children when they're alone together in the car or late at night before bed. That's an easy fallback. Jeff and I suggest couples go on date nights where the intended goal is not to talk about the kids! Instead, talk about your emotions, opinions, dreams, and goals—the stuff that you don't talk about day to day. The stuff that requires thinking. But talking and listening to each other at that level on a regular basis builds unbreakable bonds between you and another person. It can affair-proof your marriage and provide greater stability in your home life. It's something that benefits you, your spouse, and your kids.

I'm asking you to try this right now. Plan to set aside 10 minutes on five out of seven days this week to meditate on your answers to the following questions. Just think!

Questions to ask about thinking:

Are you afraid or reluctant to set aside time to "think"? Why or why not?

Are you anxious about the changes you might need to make as a result of thinking more deeply about what really matters in life? Why or why not?

Where are the best places where you can experience periods of silence?

CHAPTER FOUR

PAYING ATTENTION AND BEING KNOWN

IF YOU PUT EVEN A LITTLE OF WHAT YOU LEARN IN this chapter into practice, I promise it will start to transform every relationship you have. Think about all the ways that improved relationships add to the rest of your life—your home life, your work life, your personal life.

In this chapter I want you to start thinking about what it means to pay closer attention to yourself. There are two ultimate goals here. The first goal is for you to become more self-aware on an intimate level: your emotions, your opinions, your thoughts, your personality, your preferences. I want you to dig deep, turn over some rocks, and discover the unique details of who God designed you to be and let that truest self "be known" to others.

The second goal is something we'll tackle in a later chapter. It's about getting to know other people in a similar and intimate way. The idea is to stretch your key relationships to reach a new plateau by paying much more attention to the people closest to you—who they truly are and how they really feel. You can also include those you don't know well and/or are just acquaintances.

To get started, evaluate how well you know yourself and others by answering the following questions. Your responses will give you an idea where you are in the process. Use a scale for your responses 0-5, where 0 is "not at all" and 5 is "extremely."

____ *How well do you think you know yourself?*

____ *How well do you think others know you?*

____ *If someone wanted to buy you a meaningful gift, would it be hard for them to know what you'd want?*

____ *How well do you know your spouse's personal preferences?*

____ *How well does your best friend know your personal preferences?*

____ *How easy is it for you to make new friends?*

____ *How well do you know your top five personal needs?*

____ *How aware are you regarding the top five needs of those in your inner circle?*

____ *Are your closest relationships thriving?*

Okay, now add up your score:____. Match it to the descriptions below.

0-8 **It's a real challenge to focus and pay attention. Get out a highlighter for this chapter.**

9-18 **You're going to learn some things you've never considered.**

19-24 **You are alert to some of the ways you need to grow in this area. Get ready to learn more!**

25-34 **You're growing in your awareness of yourself and others and seeing results.**

35+ **Why are you reading this chapter? You might skip ahead!**

So, how did you do? How mindful are you? Are you paying attention to the right things? Are you paying attention at all? Start to notice these trends in yourself. Regardless of your score, I hope by now you're wondering, "If I'm going through life not paying attention like I need to, how do I get to a better place?" That's the perfect frame of mind with which to start.

LIVING IN A WORLD OF INATTENTION

The degree to which we are paying attention determines the quality of all our relationships. If we're paying attention to the right things in the right way, things go well. If not, there are consequences. People disappoint us from time to time, and we do the same to others. We inevitably sometimes fail to meet each other's expectations. Most people can point to a time when they parted ways with a friend or even a family member or when they went through a break-up with a significant other. Looking back, did you ever think something along the lines of, "Gosh, I spent so much time with this person, but it turns out they didn't even know me at all"? Being misunderstood hurts to the core, doesn't it? I'm the first one to admit that relationships are complicated, so I don't want to downplay the heartache you may have gone through. But if something like that has ever happened to you...where you invested tons of time with someone only to discover that they didn't understand you at all...there are only two explanations. Either the other person was not really paying attention to who you are—or you were not vulnerable in making your true self known.

If I asked you, "Who are you?" how would you respond? How about, "When do you feel most fulfilled and complete?" Or "What are you all about?" If you're scratching your head and thinking, "I'm not sure about the answers to these questions..." you're not alone. People routinely avoid those kinds of probing inquiries, which is why so many of our relationships lack depth and significance. I'm talking about all your close relationships—marriages, siblings, friends, and even between parents and children.

Why do we tend to avoid intimacy with those closest to us? There are many reasons. In part, it is because most people are generally unaware that they're supposed to ask those kinds of questions about life. Maybe their family wasn't close growing up. Maybe they're emotionally detached from their spouse. Maybe they've never opened up with another person about what is important to them. They don't go deep with another human being because they don't know how. I think another reason we avoid intimacy is a very practical one: we don't have time! People often don't see the point in pushing themselves to find the answers to deeper questions about significance, purpose, and meaning when the laundry still has to be done. The kids need picking up from school. The to-do list is ridiculously long, and the boss needs that marketing report first thing in the morning. What difference would having a deeper sense of knowing oneself make to everyday life? I used to wonder that same thing.

I hope to show you that the payoff is huge and your efforts are worth it. These days, I am passionate about the deeper questions because being on that purposeful journey makes me a better mother, wife, and friend. Knowing myself better elevates every relationship I have. Also, it not only helps me get through that to-do list but also helps me make a better list! Like many of you, I've spent too much time in the past avoiding myself and my feelings and my opinions. Now I go after it because I realize how much there is to learn about myself and others. And I see how much benefit I derive from the pursuit, not to mention everyone around me.

KNOWING YOURSELF

Here is what is important. You've heard it said that in order to determine where you are going, you "have to know where you've been." That's true, but I think in order to know where you're going next, you also need to know who you *are* now. Wherever you've been and wherever you go next in life, there you'll be. If you don't like yourself—or don't know yourself—it's going to be a disappointing journey. I don't want you to be another woman wandering through life never knowing who you are and why God uniquely created you. I want to know the real you! Others want to know the real you. But the question is, do *you* want to know the real you?

Again, for most of us, this is uncharted territory. Many women have rarely taken the time or invested the effort in knowing themselves. Start to prepare your heart and break up the fallow ground regarding this topic by asking yourself some of the tougher questions about your life. Don't rush through these. Contemplate each one. You may even want to journal some responses.

What are three adjectives that describe you?

What do you like about you?

What are your weaknesses?

What are you afraid of?

What are some of your goals?

What do you most want to improve about yourself?

What do you want to be known for?

LEARNING TO KNOW HOW YOU FEEL

One of the Lost Arts of Being Human that I introduced in the previous chapter is giving yourself time to think deeply. Setting aside regular times to think and ponder life makes you more connected and in tune with yourself and what you're feeling throughout the day. But now I want to focus on feelings, versus thinking. I see the difference this way: I personally enjoy *thinking*, but it takes more effort for me to know and acknowledge how I *feel*. The two are not the same. In fact, it's been a lifelong challenge for me to identify and express or even accept my own emotions.

As a young person with no emotional direction in my life, I felt deeply, but I had no one to help me understand and process those emotions. I sucked it up and developed a numbness to feelings so they wouldn't get in my way. As an adult, I learned that it's not too late to address that deficiency. Other people can teach you to process your emotions—even if you didn't have parents who knew how to ask the right questions of their child. Over the years I've progressed to a point where I can acknowledge my feelings more than I ever have. It can take me a day or two to process, depending on the circumstances, but I put in the hard work necessary to put words to whatever it is I'm feeling.

This is a common experience for many women. If someone were to ask you, "What's on your heart right now?" how easily could you answer that question? Natural caretakers, women tend to put our emotional health last while we look after everyone else sheltering under our wings. No wonder it's hard for us to put words to our feelings. Women often don't think we have time to express emotions—or even a right to do so. Scan down your entire list of priorities and you'll see your name and your needs there, just above the needs of the family dog in some cases!

Here's a recent example. When I had to leave my newest grandchild in Los Angeles and return home to Dallas a few days after he was born, it felt off. I had to unpack my emotions slowly to understand what was happening inside. I was a mix of being sad and joyful at the same time—ecstatic to meet this precious treasure but so sad to leave him, my daughter, and her husband. Because we live so far away, the miles between us make it hard to be there as much as I'd like to be.

"That's okay to feel sad," I reminded myself frequently throughout the long plane ride back to Texas. "You're allowed."

That self-talk may sound over-simplified to some, but other women know how revolutionary it is to allow yourself to express sadness, fear, anger, disappointment, anxiety, and the angst of being misunderstood. The same is true of even positive expressions like joy, peace, and playfulness. Some people have never given themselves permission to feel at all.

For so long in my early marriage and as a mom, I couldn't "do" sad. I told myself I had to step up to the plate despite how I was feeling. I worried what people would think of me if I let myself be sad. "Maybe sad doesn't look good to them," I'd conclude about my friends and family. So I became an expert at disconnecting myself from my feelings and kept going because I didn't have time or bandwidth to "go there."

So, I get it. If this chapter is making you feel uncomfortable already, that's a good sign that this is new ground you're covering. Hang in there with me.

EXERCISES TO DISCOVER THE REAL YOU

Think through another set of questions to ponder. Carefully consider your responses. And go with your gut reaction—try to hold on to the first thing you think of instead of succumbing to what you think you *should* say. Try forming your responses into full sentences, either out loud or by writing in a page of your journal if you wish.

In what area of your life are you the most intentional?

What are you passionate about and why?

What motivates you?

When was the last time you felt extremely motivated? Describe in detail how you felt.

What do you really love doing and experiencing?

What experiences, Bible verses, images, poems, books, quotes, or movies have ever resonated with you at the core of who you are? Why do you think that is?

I'm a fan of Dr. Curt Thompson and his non-profit called The Center for Being Known. He is a psychiatrist who says we all have an intrinsic desire to be known by others. He writes on his website, "The work of Being Known is not just a handful of good ideas; nor is it for any one of us to do alone. Rather, it is about joining our Creator in living an abundant life—but one that must be lived together." I highly encourage you to check out his work through his podcasts and books and maybe consider attending a conference.

Dr. Thompson notes that you must first be willing to even know who you are in order to be known. In other words, you have to do some hard work, which is what we're practicing in this book. For example, are you intuitive? Can you discern the truth in a matter? If you don't know what intuition looks like, are you at least willing to find out more about it? As a kid, I could read people really well. I wasn't a

Christian then, but I see looking back that God made me that way for a reason. When I grew older, I could ask prompting questions about someone, and the next thing I knew they were telling me their entire life story. In my thirties, I finally realized something about this uncanny ability to understand the truth about people. I have the gift of discernment, and discernment is a gift from God.

That gift, along with the other gifts God gave me—wisdom and faith—have helped me so much. God gives me wisdom to know what to say in certain situations and the faith to believe him for anything. Some of the best insights I use in Biblical marriage counseling do not come from me—they're an impression I receive from God. People will say, "How did you know that about me?" They're blown away. But I think it's just part of the gift of wisdom he gave me. He designed me to put information and insights together so that he can then point out something helpful for me to share with someone.

I also have learned I have the gift of faith. How did I patiently walk through seven long years of reconciliation with Jeff when we were divorced? God gave me extraordinary faith to believe it would happen. God had shown me early on that he was going to put my marriage back together, and he gave me the gift of faith to know this was true no matter how long it took. My friends lovingly encouraged me to move on with my life. They thought I was crazy, but for me it was easy to believe that God could do this!

Be mindful of some gift or insight or talent that comes easily for you—and how you might use it to help others. That's the power of knowing something unique about yourself. You use your gifts to help others, and you know for sure that you can't take the credit!

Life experiences accumulate over time and tell us more about ourselves and our gifts and talents. How do we access those deeper places in ourselves throughout life's seasons? It takes time. A 30-year-old might think they're self-aware. And they might be really aware for someone that age. But what about when you're 50? Then you look back and see, "Wow. I wasn't as aware as I thought I was." But that's part of the journey. We're moving along step by step.

THE BENEFITS OF KNOWING WHO YOU ARE

Part of why I want you to expand your vulnerability tolerance and get to know yourself (and let others know you) is that "being known" is a pre-requisite to being intentional about how you want to live. That just makes sense. If you have no clue who you really are, how could you know what you want to do with your life? If you don't know yourself, how can you live intentionally and make the best decisions about how you want to spend your limited time on earth?

There's no other way around it. To be intentional, you must first come to a point where you know much more about who you are on an intimate level. Being intentional means to cast aside distractions and pursue only those specific opportunities and relationships that line up with who you are becoming as a person. And then that's where the momentum builds and life grows rich! You look around and realize that you've become a passionate person who is learning to thrive!

Sum it up this way:

If you know yourself, you'll be intentional.
If you're intentional, you'll become passionate.
If you're passionate, you'll thrive.

If you're running short on intentionality and/or passion, don't worry. At least you're aware of it. Now you can do something about it.

We've covered the importance of knowing who you are, so now is a good time for me to convince you of the benefits of knowing yourself on a deeper level. Knowing yourself leads to more intentionality and easier decision-making, having more passion for what you love, and ultimately it leads to thriving.

Let's break down this formula piece by piece:

Knowing Who You Are

↓

Being Intentional

↓

Becoming Passionate

↓

Thriving

KNOWING WHO YOU ARE

The more we know ourselves, the more we're becoming a Sage—a woman of wisdom to whom others can turn for advice. No one would think that of themselves, right? We furrow our brow and say, "Me, a Sage? Who am I to give someone else advice?" Well, you may be closer to becoming one than you think, if you're willing to find out who you are at the deepest level. It's having a mindset that constantly reminds yourself, "This is a journey I'm on. I'm learning. I want to become whatever it is I'm meant to become. I want to thrive." I've processed these same concepts with hundreds of women, and all I'm doing in these pages is spelling out what this might look like for you uniquely.

BEING INTENTIONAL

Most likely, the first thing that jumps out at you when you start to know yourself better is the realization that life is short. I mean, really short. The clock is ticking. The more you know the real you, the more you fuel your ability to make better decisions about your life and everything and everyone in it. When you're done wasting your precious time trying to be someone you're not (or someone you don't even like), you are free to make better choices about how to spend the remainder of your time—and with whom, along with where, when, and why you should spend that time. That's the essence of what being intentional is about. You may change jobs. You may alter some friendships. You may sign up for some courses at the local university. When you're intentional in your approach to life, everything you do has a new purpose and that's when the next step, being passionate, comes into play.

BECOMING PASSIONATE

There are plenty of times in life when our passion for living is in short supply. We have ups and downs. That's normal. Let me be clear. In this book, I'm not talking about clinical depression or mental illness. That is a real experience for so many women and one that is outside of the scope of the strategies I'm outlying in this book and it's beyond my training. I'm a Biblical marriage counselor and not a Licensed Professional Counselor (LPC). I address the garden-variety lack of passion for living that plagues us all to varying degrees. Our kneejerk reaction when we feel down or bored is to spiral into feeling more down and more bored! I want to offer you an alternative. We all get bored, but what do you do in boredom?

When you find yourself settling for the daily drudgery of life, train yourself to recognize that you're actually in a good spot to take action. Instead of ignoring this very human and very common state, turn things around. The intense desire to "do something more with your life" can work for your benefit because it's pointing out that something is missing from your life. Learn to recognize that ache, longing, and God-given desire as the real "you" starving for passion and purpose.

It's like hunger pangs. No one has to tell you to eat when you experience physical hunger. Your stomach rumbles and you know what to do—it's dinnertime! You get something to eat and take care of that hunger until you're satisfied. Emotional hunger pangs work in the same way. They're doing you a favor, signaling to you that you need to do something about them. Everyone needs to find a focus for life that's bigger than they are. Developing all-consuming passions will help to satisfy that pain of feeling like they lack purpose. And remember the formula. Doing the hard work of knowing who you really are leads to intentionality. Being passionate comes from being intentional.

Thriving is the natural result of waking up more often than not being excited and interested in the unique opportunities ahead of you in an endless number of areas. You can deepen your spiritual relationship with God. You can immerse yourself in becoming an amazing mom. You can strengthen your friendships and devote yourself to growing as a wife. You can pursue unique opportunities in your career. You can throw yourself into learning about how you're gifted. You can become someone who thinks deeply, rests wisely, loves vulnerably, and takes care of themselves physically. Which of these most sparks your interest?

THRIVING

Thriving is hard work—don't let anyone fool you. It's not natural. And it's not easy. This "knowing yourself" business takes some effort! Again, we're not talking about Pollyanna perfection, just consistency. Still, it's risky to uncover and then face the truth about yourself, not to mention be vulnerable enough to share it with others. There's a reason why it's so difficult to get to know people on an intimate level. As humans, our guard is up and we don't naturally take the risk and open ourselves up to one another. Deep, rich, satisfying friendships and relationships don't just come along and happen without significant effort. But when we put in the effort, it's like experiencing an upgrade in every area of life.

A PLAN OF ACTION: EXPLORE AND TRAIN

Getting to know yourself is like hiking up a steep mountain. For one thing, you don't do it in one day. It's vital to set realistic expectations for this process from the beginning. Realize that it's a lifelong journey ahead of you and get comfortable with the idea that it will be a while, if ever, before you reach the top. You're just going from plateau to plateau, learning the whole way. I've been at this a while, and it still surprises me that I'm constantly learning new things about myself! So here's a plan of action you can put into place when you're ready to summit to the next plateau of getting to know yourself better.

EXPLORE

Stop and think about any negative emotions you're experiencing when you're going through difficulty. What do they look like? Instead of overmedicating, or over-exercising, or denying something has happened to make you feel this way, take a look at it. Kids are a great cover up for not exploring our emotions. As moms, we stay busy and don't deal with stuff. It's never-ending. I always say that small kids are physically demanding and older (even adult) kids are emotionally demanding. It's like Jeff used to say when our girls were teenagers, "What are they crying about *now*?"

Many studies show that when we hold things inside and don't explore our emotions, they fester. When we don't express it, explore it, and deal with it, it still comes out somewhere in the mind and body. We end up with sickness, anxiety, anger, disappointment, fear. Post Traumatic Stress Disorder (PTSD) is not just limited to the battlefield. It happens to everyday people in everyday life.

Dr. Daniel Amen is a popular brain specialist with clinics all over the country. My family is familiar with his work. He has taken pictures of the human brain from many angles to demonstrate that there are "holes" that result inside the brain after trauma. It's possible to heal these tender spaces if you learn helpful strategies to deal in a healthy way with the emotional fall-out from the painful periods of life. We can all benefit from his research. There is resulting trauma from a literal injury, but trauma also results from intangible injuries from abuse, neglect, tough relationships, divorce, illness, an accident—all kinds of situations. And here's the thing. It doesn't go away on its own. It stays in your brain until we deal with it.

Exploring your emotions, as difficult as doing so may be, gives you back your freedom. However, people who have been traumatized by something that happened in their lives often don't see it that way. They want to stuff it down and ignore it and just get on with it. It's even possible not to realize trauma has occurred because oftentimes it's not something tangible you are aware of, so you're ignorant of how it's affecting you. I can't remember a lot of my childhood because I've blocked it out. It wasn't until my early fifties that I completely understood why.

Others may say, "I don't really need to go to counseling. What will I talk about?" A good counselor can pull it out of you. There are a lot of bad counselors too. How do you find a good one? You can ask people for references, but just because Betty loved her counselor doesn't mean you will also. Book a session with a new counselor and see if the two of you click. If not, you might need to move on to another one.

Jesus wants us to be transformed and not stay the way we are. He wants us to be free, which is a theme the Bible talks about frequently—even more than you might realize. Here are just a few verses to show you what I mean. I could include many, many more, but you get the idea.

> For freedom Christ has set us free; stand firm therefore, and do not submit again to a yoke of slavery.
> *Galatians 5:1*

> Now the Lord is the Spirit, and where the Spirit of the Lord is, there is freedom.
> *2 Corinthians 3:17*

> So if the Son sets you free, you will be free indeed.
> *John 8:36*

> And you will know the truth, and the truth will set you free.
> *John 8:32*

> For you were called to freedom, brothers.
> *Galatians 5:13*

Freedom is what we're looking for when we start to explore our past and how it affects who we are. When we find ourselves experiencing damaging and limiting emotions that are holding us back, we must take the next step.

TRAIN

After you have explored your feelings during a particular season in life, take some sort of action. Have a plan in place when you experience emotional pangs. It doesn't have to be a big deal; just put something you've learned into practice. Schedule a coffee with a friend to talk you through it. Set aside time to grow still, meditate, and pray in the evening for a few extra minutes. Make time to read a devotional book and some scriptures before you go to bed or when you get up, first thing in the morning. Go to God's Word. It's a spiritual issue at its root, even though you're processing on an emotional level.

We can all fall down rabbit holes and get stuck emotionally. Training involves learning to encourage yourself and asking God to help you. The more habits you develop to retrain your thinking when you feel down, the more you will know what to do when you find yourself struggling emotionally. These skills become imbedded common knowledge, and implementing them comes more naturally the more you do it. You have to remember one thing: our bodies can only do so much; and our body includes our brain. We are mental, emotional, physical, and spiritual beings. So we have to nurture all those unique parts of us. There's no cookie cutter plan of action for everybody, another reminder of how important it is to know yourself and what works for you.

Sometimes training involves reading more about how to deal with emotions. Some of you will benefit from reading a book by Dr. Curt Thompson, as I've mentioned, and there are many additional resources and authors out there like Paul David Tripp, Pete Scazzero and his *Emotionally Healthy* series, and Debra Fileta, author of *Are You Really Okay?*.

Sometimes training involves going to counseling, for intense seasons or just for a tune-up to check in with yourself. You can process with a qualified counselor things like, "Why am I so fearful? What holds me back?" We all had experiences in our childhood that affect us today—for good and bad. Every person. How do I know that? Because none of us had perfect parents. And that's why I'm talking about the importance of being known, especially to yourself, so you can explore, "Why do I do certain things like...?"

There are also free and sliding-scale resources available in your community, including churches who may sponsor programs such as Celebrate Recovery. Celebrate Recovery is a Christian-based recovery program that deals with hurts, habits, and hang-ups, and many people have found freedom and healing there.

A WORD ABOUT DISCERNMENT

The other part about knowing yourself is knowing who and what you follow regarding advice. The toughest part about gathering resources like counselors and books and programs is to determine what they offer. For example, discernment is a big deal for me regarding my podcast, including the people I choose to interview and what topics I lean into regarding the topic of thriving. I work very hard to keep a spiritually and Biblically-centered focus on my podcast. Discernment is a keen sense of perception when I'm reviewing potential guests that helps me protect my listeners, my values, and my focus.

My filter is the Word of God, and I can say by experience that I've found it to be very effective in my life. Learning to read the Bible was like removing blinders from my eyes. I couldn't believe I had missed out on this for so long! Bible study was a new avenue I had never traveled before, and I needed other Christians walking alongside me to show me what the Bible was all about. It was exciting, and I developed such a passion for God's Word. I felt as if I couldn't get enough. Thirty years in, I feel the same way; it has never waned. If you haven't already done so, I encourage you to explore the Bible; you may find the same to be true for you.

PRACTICING THE LOST ARTS OF BEING HUMAN

THE LOST ART OF PAYING ATTENTION

We move through life and don't notice it. Most of us go through our days and we miss the important stuff happening all around us because we're not paying attention to the right things. How aware are you throughout your day? Or are you just kind of making your way through life? Is the reason you don't feel like you're thriving because you're really not paying attention?

Everyone's different. Not everyone has the same capacity to get through daily life—and have leftover energy to look under the surface for things like where God is working, who needs more attention, etc. For example, I can multitask and get a lot of things done at once. And I don't necessarily mean tasks like dusting or cleaning the bathrooms. I mean thinking and writing. When I'm working on several writing or work projects at one time, I don't feel pressured by that at all. In fact, sometimes I am more effective because of the busyness, and I prefer to have a lot going on. Then you have someone like Jeff, who doesn't do well with any kind of multitasking. He prefers handling just one thing at a time and that's an equally effective strategy for him. There are different personalities. You have to know "you." And then you can move to what paying attention looks like for you in different areas of your unique life.

Cultivating the Lost Art of Paying Attention means taking new steps. The first big step is simply being self-aware. There is a lot of fine tuning on an individual level to become more self-aware—and it takes hard work. This is a journey of continual awareness. We have to keep in mind that variables are constantly changing all around us, too. It's that whole "seasons of life" thing that keeps us on our toes. Everything from our health to our family dynamics are vulnerable to change in an instant. Our awareness has to keep up the pace so that we make sure we're always learning new things about ourselves as we go in and out of life's cycles and seasons.

Questions about knowing yourself:

Do you stop on a regular basis and assess your emotions during the day?

For the next week, pause daily at least once and ask yourself, "What things are distracting me today? And how are they possibly affecting me and my ability to pay attention to and listen to others?" What did you learn doing this exercise?

Questions about knowing others:

Do you often find yourself being distracted or half-listening in a conversation?

Do you regularly tune people out—consciously or intentionally? If so, why?

Do you consistently listen and try to understand what others are saying?

What does active listening look like, in your opinion? Who do you know that does this really well?

Part of being aware and paying attention to deeper things is also kind of like listening to the Holy Spirit. Can you hear the voice of God? I've never heard his voice audibly. But I can point to different times in my life when I felt guided.

Questions you may have about hearing God:

How do I know it's God and not my own thoughts?

How do I learn to recognize God's voice more and more?

How do I know when God is speaking to me?

CHAPTER FIVE

CAUTION: PITFALLS AND BLIND SPOTS AHEAD!

FAIR WARNING, WHEN YOU START TO FOCUS ON thriving, you will likely encounter resistance along the way. There are pitfalls as well as sharp curves and blind corners along the journey. I've loved all the seasons I have gone through so far, even though some have been excruciatingly painful and hard. No one escapes the tough parts of life. In fact, the Bible says pointedly, "*When* you encounter trials of many kinds..." It's not "if" you encounter them—it's "when," because they come into everyone's life. I am so grateful for how God has always remained steady, helping me along and even carrying me sometimes through the worst parts!

Let's get refocused on the purpose of the trials and challenges we face, especially since hardship is inevitable.

What if we take a different spin and learn to use these events and situations to grow and mature us into the woman God wants us to be? Remember, I'm advocating consistency, not perfection, as the guiding definition of what it means to thrive. Finding out what situations, habits, relationships, and trials trip you up and make you inconsistent is helpful information!

In this chapter, I'll walk through some of the more common pitfalls and blind spots that tend to throw us off our game and discourage our desire and ability to thrive. Guilt from our past, jealousy, comparison to others, self-sabotage, compromise, resentment, crises—these things threaten our progress, stunt our growth, and can even paralyze us. The list is long and could be a whole book in itself! I've chosen some of the more common and significant topics I've seen hinder other women and keep them from thriving.

PITFALL: BEING TOO HARD ON OURSELVES

Sometimes, for example, we don't take into account the season of life we're in when we try something new outside of our comfort zones. It can be a blind spot because we don't see the situation we're in properly. The ministry I've created for women helps tighten that gap between the goals they have for themselves—spiritually, emotionally, physically, mentally, relationally—and what they're actually accomplishing. If I can help you succeed in making small steps toward solid progress, you're more likely to continue to set realistic goals. But if you take on too much too soon and fail, then you won't even try thriving anymore.

Let me give a personal example. The hardest season in

motherhood for me was when I had small children at home. When their kids are not in school full time, mothers literally don't have a lot of extra time. I remember that season well and how much it would have meant to me if someone had encouraged me to give myself grace back then because I was in a hard season. I desperately wanted to thrive as a mom and take advantage of every opportunity, but I put too much pressure on myself to do so. It would have been a relief if someone had reminded me that I didn't have to do motherhood perfectly to thrive. I didn't have to do everything exactly right to be a good mom. It's not all or nothing when it comes to thriving. You can apply this principle of giving yourself grace across the board, no matter what stage of life you're in. What I want you to do is to know yourself well enough to realize what's hindering you and then call on one or more of the strategies you're learning to get past it.

PITFALL: BEING SOCIALLY UNAWARE

You're learning a lot about the importance of being personally and socially aware in this book. Personally aware means knowing yourself, but what does social awareness mean to you? Sometimes I've found it's easier to understand a fuzzy concept by knowing its opposite. Being socially "unaware" probably (and unfortunately) describes the majority of us. And by "us" I mean busy wives, singles, moms, and businesswomen with limited bandwidth. Socially unaware people are around others and think mainly of themselves. It's not because they have bad intentions. "Self" is just the default mindset for most people.

What does that preoccupation look like? Instead of

brainstorming creative ways to engage others, socially unaware people focus primarily on how insecure they feel about their own conversation skills. They worry about not having anything to say and are pre-occupied about who is or is not going to be at an event for them to talk to.

According to my dictionary, "unaware" can even be ignorant, inconsiderate, inattentive, neglectful, insensitive, prideful, and unfriendly. (Ouch! I stopped reading after "insensitive...") Not surprisingly, "unaware" also has a propensity to be rude. Socially unaware people also interrupt others frequently by habit. Unable to "read the room," they remain unaware of other people's stories, their emotions, their experiences, or their background.

On the other hand, being socially aware means I am interested and attuned to those around me in social situations, instead of being hyper-focused on myself. Seeking to be understood is one of the fundamental needs of every human, maybe even greater than the need for love. George Orwell made that comparison when he wondered, "Perhaps one did not want to be loved so much as understood." What a gift we give to others when we make a conscious effort to think more of others and how we can engage and understand them. Being socially aware means I listen more than I talk and seek to understand, not insist on being understood by everyone.

Which is it for you—are you socially unaware or aware? This is a big blind spot for most people and they really have to think about which one they are. One easy way you can start to evaluate your own social awareness is to think about how you go about giving gifts to others. It's really that simple.

How do you decide on a gift for someone? For example, the last thing I want to do is find a parking spot in a crowded mall parking lot and drag myself into an even more crowded mall to buy a gift. I prefer smaller boutique shops because a curated set of gifts often gets closer to expressing how I feel about someone. I may even give them a gift card to one of their favorite restaurants. That shows I know something about their likes and dislikes. It's not just a random gift I picked out to cross it off my list.

How do you typically pick out a gift for someone you love? Do you usually start with something that you would like? Does it take forever to think of something? Or can you say that you know the person so well that it's easy for you to identify something you know they will enjoy? That's called being thoughtful and intentional. Gifts are a creative way to say we know and understand the people closest to us. The opposite is just as true. Have you ever received a gift from a loved one and thought immediately, "I don't really care for this"? First, you wonder if you can return it without a receipt. Then the sinking realization dawns on you, "They obviously don't know me at all, or they would never think of this for me."

Or have you ever felt as if someone bought you something on the fly or out of obligation, without giving much thought to it other than to say they "gave" you something? It's a terrible feeling, especially if it's your spouse, one of your kids, or a close friend who should know you better than anyone. How do you avoid doing this same thing to others? When you figure that out, you'll step aside when you see this pitfall on your path and not fall into it.

PITFALL: NOT CARING ABOUT OTHERS

Selfishness is the antithesis to thriving, and it will hold you back tremendously. How well do you listen with empathy? Empathy means to share and understand another person's feelings. We must listen well in order to fully engage in a conversation. By listening well to another person, you can often sense their struggle long before they tell you what's wrong. Practice this skill often and you'll see what I mean. Do you listen more than you speak in a typical conversation? Do you have a bad habit of interrupting someone during a conversation?

Does listening always have to be done with our ears? No. You can challenge yourself to listen for someone's tone of voice. Try to capture their feelings (what's going on in their heart) at the same time that you hear their words. Don't try to process their words all in your mind. Sometimes we try to make what someone is saying fit a pre-determined idea of what we think they mean. Anyone can listen using their ears. But a relationally thriving person has developed a secret skill of listening with a heart full of compassion, empathy, and love for the other person.

I try to pay attention to what someone is saying by hearing not only their words but also listening carefully for their intention behind those words. Think about it. Are you able to "hear" a friend, spouse, or family member's emotions? Their fears? Their concerns? Or are you sometimes waiting them out just so you can respond or even pounce on them and defend yourself if necessary?

In any type of relationship—acquaintance, friend, family, or stranger—always remember that listening goes both ways! What we say next after someone confides in us is important. We must listen well to be able to respond well with our words and body language. If we haven't listened and truly heard what they're saying with their words and their body language, our advice is likely to be ill-timed and off-target.

Have you ever thought about how your listening skills can hold you back relationally? Instead, you can work on those skills and learn to benefit another person in so many ways just by listening better. If I am listening attentively to someone, it's usually because they listen well to me and I want to return the favor. We gain respect when we listen well, and we have more respect for the other person too! What happens inside of you when you feel respected? How do you feel when you are aware that you've listened well?

PITFALL: COMPARISON

This is a biggie. In fact, I saw this quote recently on Instagram: "There's only one cure to comparison living, and that is contentment!" So true! We spend much emotional, spiritual, mental, and physical energy comparing ourselves to someone we think we "should" be rather than being content with our progress. What if we invested more into getting to know and nurture the woman God is already making? He is always molding and shaping us and making all things new, yet we hardly perceive it.

For instance, if I like someone's hair, or an outfit that looks super cute on someone, or they have a talent that I'm curious about, I try to find out more or learn about what it is. Then I think about how it may or may not work for me.

I desire to develop my own style and be confident in myself! I don't want to look like someone else. I don't want to dress like someone else. For sure, I don't want to be someone else. I am at my best when I nurture and grow "me" instead and understand who God has made me!

So let's look deeply into ourselves and ask some tough questions. Who are you comparing yourself to and why? What is it you desire that you don't have, but you think will make you happy? You were created in God's image, and he has an amazing purpose for you. Do you have any idea what your gifts and purpose might be?

I looked up the definition of "comparison" in the dictionary and also its antonym (opposite).

Comparison: likeness, measuring, resemblance
Antonym of comparison: conformity, copy, dissension

Such opposites. Conformity, copying and dissension. Reading those words puts a frown on my face, brings me down, and causes a heaviness inside of me. Why is that? Because God has created each of us in a unique and wonderful way and wants to set us free from comparing! I take being God's creation very seriously. Think about it for a minute. Each person is made uniquely *by him for his purposes*. What an honor, right? Can we stretch our minds and hearts to embrace this mindset?

If only we could wrap our brains around our uniqueness. The secret to not comparing yourself is not telling yourself not to compare. It's focusing on something positive instead, such as the unique creation you are. If we did this more often, I think our comparison bucket would be virtually non-existent. I have such a heart for women who constantly feel they don't measure up. They truly are not thriving in life.

PITFALL: FEELING OVERWHELMED OR STUCK

Busyness is often the culprit behind this roadblock to thriving. Women play a lot of roles, depending on where they are in life. And most women can multi-task fairly well. The danger is getting in a rut when crossing off items on our to-do lists at home and/or at the office. We feel we are on a treadmill and can't get off. For example, there are seasons at home when moms do laundry and run after little kids all day long. There are people at the office who feel overwhelmed by all they must accomplish to satisfy their boss. Those who are married may struggle with finding time for each other because they're too busy, and by the time they get home, they just want to lie on the couch and binge watch TV.

We have to do something to get ourselves un-stuck. Thinking outside the box and focusing on new thoughts can throw you off-center when you're numb, feeling as if you're not thriving. Get creative in your solutions. To those who have children—what did you think life would be like when you decided to have children? Reframe your feelings of frustration to focus instead on being grateful for the amazing child/children you have. Soak in the high calling of raising and nurturing them. To those who are married—I understand that you're both busy and tired at night. Sometimes a special dinner date can take place right there in your living room after the kids are in bed. Single people who are not thriving relationally can sign up for a class or lecture on something of interest. You'll meet like-minded people and challenge yourself to get out of your routine.

Ask yourself: What does feeling "stuck" mean to me? How do I feel stuck? The feeling of paralysis or numbness is a different experience for everyone; we don't have the same journey. Some women might say, "I feel stuck because I have to work five days a week." Others might say, "I feel stuck because I wanted to be a stay-at-home mom, but my family needs another income." Sometimes we're stuck emotionally and feel as if we can't gain any traction on dealing with the issues we know we have. Why are these still plaguing us after all this time? That frustration can make you unwilling to try reaching another level in your everyday life. What's the point?

Here are some other questions to consider: Am I aware of it when I'm stuck? Am I really stuck? Or am I being lazy and making excuses for not continuing in my thriving journey? Think about this also—when do you most often get stuck? Is there a certain time of the year, like wintertime, when you might be more prone to depression and listlessness? Or the holidays? Or an anniversary of a trauma, someone you lost, or the date of your divorce? Focusing on the negative—such as your age and the aging process—can distract you from living with gratitude.

Do you blame anyone or anything for your stuck-ness? I hear women confess that they want out of their marriage more often than you would believe. The tendency is to blame the husband for this or that. I know we're making progress when instead someone eventually points the finger at themselves and asks, "What responsibility do I have for the distressing state of my marriage? My unhealthy relationships with my family? My depressing situation?" That's how you get un-stuck, right there. Believing you can take some action, however small, on yourself, your relationships, your job, and your parenting is empowering.

PITFALL: HURTFUL PEOPLE

People can sabotage you to keep you from thriving—either purposefully or subconsciously. You do realize that some people won't encourage or support you in your efforts to thrive, right? They don't want you to reach the next level of abundance in your life for fear that you'll leave them behind. Or because they're jealous. Or because they're stuck and they want you to be stuck, too. This kind of negativity can waft over your life like a dark cloud and do real damage to your self-esteem. It can come from a co-worker, a friend, a spouse, a parent, a child—you name it. I've seen it all and I've experienced some of it personally too.

At the risk of being vulnerable, I'm sharing the following excerpt from my journal when an episode of "hurtful people" happened to me. Don't think because I'm writing this book that this kind of stuff never happens to me. It does, so I can empathize with anyone who feels this way!

> *I'm still processing what happened the other day (a sunny April day in 2018) and unfortunately have had to set some boundaries. I can be "surface" and not share my heart if I don't want to and don't feel safe. So, the safety net was broken. This time bad. To the point where I'm not going back to where I was before in this relationship. I have plenty of people to share my heart with—my excitement, my struggles,*

and joys. I can just be myself without any judgment and just receive their support, love, openness, and peace. Yep, peace. I have people in my life who give me peace, and it's those I will gravitate to. I'm heard. I can be me, warts and all. Perfection was once my livelihood, and that did me in. So the people who make me feel as if I need to be perfect are now taking a back seat to those with whom I'm accepted and not living under a microscope.

God wants me to have a peaceful spirit, even in the challenges of life. His goal is thriving! He wants me to be dependent on him and not focused on what others' opinions and goals are for me. I need to know "me" well enough to live this out and allow God to mold and shape me—and not be so worried about others.

I'm an admirer—but I need to guard myself on the people I admire and how much. I want to notice when I'm being drawn off-sides. God calls me to guard my heart because it is the wellspring of life. Is my heart guardable? Where am I vulnerable to hurt, and where is my heart left unprotected? What do I do about this?

It takes strength to guard your heart. It takes discipline and boundaries. It takes choices—and then follow-through. It takes desire.

So the balance for me is this: living out the Christian life as a follower of Jesus....and yet knowing yourself deeply to know how others (and myself) can sabotage a thriving life. Jesus came to give me life and life abundant (to the full). So what does that mean for me? It means being well-supplied, of the maximum size, filled to utmost capacity, and complete. Amen!

BUILDING YOUR RESERVES INSTEAD OF FALLING INTO A PIT

I love when women can be vulnerable, honest, and real while sharing the hard stuff about their lives. Here are some of the staples that keep me from getting distracted and off track.

FAITH

I think you know by now that faith in Jesus is my life. He is Life, Love, and Strength to me. I became a Jesus follower when he picked me up off the floor after a very traumatic season in my life, and he penetrated my heart at such a deep level that it's hard to describe. But Jesus saved me from the mess and put me on the right path. It brings me to tears even now as I reflect on all he has done in me, my marriage, my family, and in my life. So it comes as no surprise that I still do the very same thing today that I started doing all those years ago—setting my alarm each morning to wake up to hang out with Jesus. It is by far the richest part of my day! Hanging out with Jesus is the best medicine you can find when you feel stuck, unloved, desperate, lonely—all the things that keep us from thriving!

FOCUSING ON WHAT MATTERS TO ME

How do I keep centered and confident in a world where beauty, looks, and success can get us women off course super quickly? Fashion, style, and brands are fun. But I think what's important is developing your own style! I've done that since I was little girl. I'd study fashion in magazines (we didn't have the Internet!) and then decide what a good look would be for me. I often say, "I want to grow old gracefully!" That means I want to dress in a classy, feminine, elegant way and never compromise being a godly woman in this area of my life.

Above all, health is what really matters to me. I find when I focus on being healthy from the inside out, I'm not as consumed with the external me. I have always been a health nut and love being an all-natural kind of woman. Since I can remember, I have eaten clean (lots of veggies, nuts, grass-fed meat, pasture-raised chicken and eggs, as well as wild-caught fish). Working out, taking care of my mind as well as my spirit, and keeping abreast of who God has made me spiritually, emotionally, physically, sexually, and professionally, is by far a must for me. Now that I'm older, all that effort has served me well. It has been totally worth it. I will continue to do this until the day I die because I feel young and vibrant, even at this stage of the game.

REDEFINING MY RELATIONSHIP TO SOCIAL MEDIA

Do you have a love/ hate relationship with social media? Gosh, I do! Our social media culture is affecting us women more than we would like to admit and in so many different ways. Have you thought about how true that is, even while scrolling through your feed? Even if it's a subconscious thing, we all struggle with comparing ourselves to others in more ways than we think.

Don't get me wrong; I love social media. I have to work very hard at not being addicted, but I love people, care about their lives, and love what I learn from them! But if we are not careful, we often compare ourselves way too much to others' lives, looks, clothes, bodies, and work. It whittles away at our hearts, and it can be the destroyer of them, if we allow it.

But I refuse to let that happen to me. I refuse because God refuses. I will not allow my joy to be stolen and stomped on because of the false messages social media can portray. Not all messages are false, but the filter we personally use, and the lens through which we see ourselves can be a catalyst to insecurity, comparison, jealousy, and strife. And God loathes this. I want you to dig deep and really ask yourself the hard questions about where you stand with social media.

Might I stick my neck out please? It seems as if every book I read lately talks about how social media is bad for you! I don't want to be another voice crying out against social media, especially when I believe it's hard and possibly unrealistic to think we can ignore social media or cut it out of our lives completely. Some people advocate "social media fasting," and there's nothing wrong with that. I do think it's possible to practice some form of rationing and re-evaluating our relationships with social media. Maybe you'll find your relationship is balanced—maybe you'll find a few tweaks you could make to ensure it's not taking away from your think-time or having a harmful impact on your relationships.

That said, my opinion of social media is that if used properly, it can actually grow and stretch us in the most positive of positives! That is if we try to learn something from social media instead and refuse to allow the habit of comparison to secure a foothold in our hearts. When we prioritize really understanding who Jesus is and what he has done for us, we are free to utilize social media for all the positive ways it can enhance our lives, not hinder them!

PRACTICING THE LOST ARTS OF BEING HUMAN

Trials and challenges are hard and can even be de-humanizing. By that I mean we feel beat up emotionally and spiritually and mentally—even physically. We're bruised and worn out and feeling disconnected. So, the following Lost Arts I want to suggest are simple, refreshing steps you can take to re-enter life and start to fill your emotional and relational tank again.

THE LOST ART OF SHARING MEALS

Food is not just fuel for the body, although the type of food you put in your body is vital and important. Food, however, is much more than that for a thriving person. It is a way to improve relationships and bring us closer to those we love. Making and serving food connects us to others and ourselves as we prepare it. We can potentially relax while enjoying it. Research has even shown that people feel happier sharing meals with family and friends. As a bonus, it's a proven fact that good conversation during a meal is also distracting and keeps us from eating too much! We're more likely to stay at a normal weight when we converse with others as we eat.

Think about the last few meals you ate. Were you alone when you ate? Were you in front of the TV while you ate, even with your spouse or family? Sometimes I see couples out to eat and they never speak to each other. They may play on their phones throughout the meal until the waitress brings their check and it's time to go home. We've lost the art of sharing meals and what it can do for our souls to come together with friends and family and break bread. Sometimes we hesitate to ask others over for dinner at our home because we're embarrassed and fear company will judge us. Some people have lost the art of sharing meals because they never learned to entertain in the first place! I remember one Thanksgiving 20 years ago when I was working my butt off in the kitchen preparing the *perfect* meal and setting the *perfect* table for the four of us. Meanwhile, my girls and their dad were laughing, dancing, and cutting up in the living room without a care in the world. Finally, I let them know how stressed I was, and one of my girls asked me, "Mom, do you ever enjoy the holidays?" Ooof. Man. That set me back. What was I teaching my kids? It was a defining moment that changed the trajectory of how I entertain. I no longer strive for a perfect meal or perfect table—I want everyone to have fun and enjoy meals at our home. And that includes me.

If you're feeling burned out, stressed, overwhelmed, stuck, or in any other stage of emotional distress, try recovering the Lost Art of Sharing Meals. You may soon find that your soul—as well as your body—is being nourished at every meal.

Questions to ask about sharing meals:

When you think about sharing meals with others, what immediately comes to mind?

What do you enjoy about it?

What are you worried about?

Who are you trying to impress? Why?

Are you trying to be perfect? If so, why?

What does perfection mean to you?

If you feel stressed at the thought of preparing and sharing a meal, what are you actually stressed about?

What about this experience would make you feel a sense of calm instead?

THE LOST ART OF BEING AT HOME

When the pandemic hit, the Lost Art of Being at Home gained worldwide attention and significance. We all spent much more time at home during that extended period. But what did you learn about yourself and your home during this experience? Is your house the kind of home you want it to be? Are you very domestic? If you worked from home, did you enjoy working out of your house? Do you like piddling around in the kitchen, garden, or yard?

"Home" is an emotion-filled word that touches the deepest part of us. The traditional idea is that home is to be a respite—a place where people feel loved, safe, connected, comfortable, and at peace. This is especially important because, as we've discussed throughout this chapter, life is hard on all of us at different times.

What transforms an ordinary house into a home? What effort does it require? Being at home is our opportunity to take care of something special to enrich our lives and the lives of others. No matter if you live alone, are an empty nester, or have a family and kids at home, you have the opportunity to welcome guests into your home. What do they feel when they walk in? Do they feel comfortable and cozy? If you live at home with your family, what do they experience there? Peace or utter chaos?

The question for all of us to consider is: How do you create a home, instead of just having a "house"? People have often commented on how calming our home is. There is a reason for that. I play soft, usually instrumental music in my home to set the tone for peace and relaxation. I light candles. We often have fresh food cooking in the kitchen, which smells so good and welcoming.

As a busy society, I fear we're losing touch with the Lost Art of Being at Home. We're losing the cozy, warm, hospitable place it's meant to be and just settling for a place where we sleep and watch Netflix. A chaotic, neglected home creates nervous energy. It's tense and unsettling. And often it's cold and sterile with no "life" in it.

Thriving has a lot to do with feeling rooted and grounded—your home can be that place for you. On the surface, I have a busy life. If you looked at my calendar, that's what you'd conclude. But let me tell you something that grounds and roots me. I recently brought home 10 baby succulent plants from a nursery. Those little guys gave me so much joy when I planted them. I couldn't wait to go outside each day and check on them, even if all I needed to do was pull a few weeds. I was following my heart, digging in the soil, and doing something at home I love to do. What slow-down-and-be-present kind of activity accomplishes that for you at home? Have you noticed what slow-down-and-be-present kinds of activities your family enjoys at home? What are you doing to encourage their sense of connection to home?

Questions to ask about being at home:

When you think of making a home, rather than a house, what does that mean to you?

What could you do to bring more warmth to your home?

What could bring more peace, tranquility, and calm? How could you reduce the chaos?

What about your home encourages joy, versus stress?

Is there any distress, misery, or sadness associated with being at home now? Why is that?

What might make your home more charming and inviting? What might make it feel more alive?

Would others say your home feels delightful, comforting, and refreshing? Why or why not?

CHAPTER SIX

THE WILDERNESS IS REAL

TWO MONTHS AFTER MY DIVORCE WAS FINAL, TO MY surprise, I became a Christian. I grew up Catholic, and I'm so thankful for the foundation my parents gave me about God. The problem was, I didn't know about a personal relationship with Jesus, and I was never told that I could study the Bible myself. As an adult, I thought about God from time to time. But when I became a Christian, everything was different. I hadn't realized before that the Bible was so valuable, and now it became the guidebook for my life! Suddenly, I realized I didn't have to go so far as ending my marriage. Not only that, but I also began to have the sense that God wanted me to reconcile with my husband.

This realization came about because I started studying what the Bible says about marriage and God's plan for couples. I was learning how to journal and seek daily direction and guidance from God. Ironically, this dramatic shift also marked the start of my wilderness experience, a bewildering seven-year journey that began after the judge granted the divorce I'd thought I desperately wanted.

If you've ever tasted the grit of your own mistakes or felt lost and alone in a desperate situation, you know what it's like to be in a wilderness. The wilderness experience is real and it happens many times throughout life. The wilderness is getting fired from your job when it wasn't your fault; it's a breakup out of the blue; it's a sudden drop in income; it's a disability after an accident; it's a divorce, a death, depression. The wilderness takes many forms, but all involve a great deal of waiting. In the dark. When you don't know what's going to happen next. When the way is unclear.

In my case, there was a possibility that my marriage had a *small* chance of being restored. Very small. As likely as someone making their way out of a wilderness alone. The odds were against me. There was no guarantee that God would allow me to remarry Jeff someway, somehow. With no idea how to start a reconciliation process, I blindly made my way down an unknown path. God made it very clear to me during my journaling/prayer time that I was now in a wilderness. If I wanted to get through it, I had to focus on him and get out of his way so he could work. I also had to do whatever I could to give him the glory while I went forward by faith.

Thankfully, whenever I felt especially uncertain about the next step, God gave me eyes to see and ears to hear from him. Understandably, Jeff wasn't so ready to reconcile. The hurt I caused him was overwhelming. It seemed ridiculous at points to ask God for such an impossibility. After all, I am just an ordinary person like anyone else. So why should I expect a miracle? But I was learning that God is supernatural, and God does supernatural things through ordinary people. So, I told myself, why not ask him for the miraculous?

I love how my friend Christine Caine says it, "Impossible is where God starts; miracles are what God does!" As I fiercely studied my Bible for the first time, I began to realize a pattern. God often performed miracles when and where they were least expected. Over time, I learned to take two verses very seriously. One is Ephesians 3:20, "God can do immeasurably more than you could ever ask or imagine..." and "Nothing is impossible with God" (Matthew 19:26). At this point, I could not imagine God taking something so broken and putting the pieces back together. And yet, that phrase right from the Bible, "nothing is impossible," is so definitive. *Nothing....nothing is impossible.* No matter what you are facing, and we are all facing something, my story is evidence that God can do the impossible in the wilderness.

The goal is to THRIVE, not just survive, the pain and heartache that inevitably comes our way. We have to start somewhere, and it's not always easy to figure out where! So let's break down the word THRIVE into an acronym that will help you create an action plan to use in the wilderness:

T-Wait on God's **Timing**

H-Live with a new **Heart**

R-**Remind** yourself you are loved

I-Be **Interested** in what God is interested in (and expect to be **Interrupted**)

V-Become a **Victor**, not a victim

E-**Expect** God to show up

I learned something new with every step of this acronym. It was my map through the wilderness. This process wasn't days. It wasn't months. But many long years of slogging my way through it. This is my story of how I learned to THRIVE in a seven-year journey through the wilderness and came out the other side. Do you believe that can happen in your life?

T- WAIT ON GOD'S TIMING

The more I learn from the Bible, the more I see that timing and waiting are major themes for all of God's people. This was the case when Moses led the Hebrew people out of their bondage in Egypt straight into many years of wilderness and eventually to the Promised Land. The Bible describes the journey in Exodus 13:17-18:

> When Pharaoh finally let the people go, God did not lead them along the main road that runs through Philistine territory, *even though that was the shortest route* to the Promised Land. God said, "If the people are faced with a battle, they might change their minds and return to Egypt." So God led the people in a roundabout way [the long way around] through the wilderness toward the Red Sea.

Gosh, God. You know a shorter way? But you take us through the wilderness first? Why? We grumble and complain about the wilderness with good reason! Nothing is clear in those times, and we feel lost. We instinctively want the quickest route out, but here's the thing. God knew the shorter route was the harder path and the Hebrews weren't ready for it. The shorter path would mean fighting major battles and engaging fierce enemies. They weren't a professional army; they were former slaves! Of course their natural inclination would have been to turn around and head back to Egypt at the first sign of trouble. So God had them take the long road to the Promised Land instead.

Wait. Couldn't God have saved some major time and heartache by getting them to the Promised Land sooner? And while we're on that topic, why didn't God intervene in my life *before* I got divorced? The timing seemed backwards. If I had been writing this script, I would have had the life-changing encounter with God *before* our divorce court date. My initial plan for restoring my marriage was about 6.5 years shorter than God's plan. But I wouldn't have been ready for reconciliation then. And neither would Jeff. We have no idea what God is protecting us from, or teaching us, by taking us the long way around in our wilderness.

Once you are willing to believe and accept that everything happens according to God's timing, not yours, your perspective changes. For the better. When we realize that God created every person for himself and for his glory, not for us and for our glory, we're in a better position to THRIVE! When life becomes solely about us, it's harder to THRIVE. We're weighed down with our own control issues and expectations for all our relationships and circumstances. We want everything to go according to plan, our plan. However, when you receive the gracious gift of finally understanding that life is not about you, your eyes are opened. At least that's how it felt for me. God supernaturally helped me to accept his perfect timing for everything going on in my life! That's not to say that waiting for something I really wanted was anything less than brutal.

H - LIVE WITH A NEW HEART

I had a marriage problem. More than that, I had a heart problem. Getting a divorce was easy; getting through the wilderness would be a long journey. The old me—the heart of who I was the first 30 years of my life—simply wouldn't be able to make the trip. My old heart was the one that had rescued myself from bulimia by sheer will and determination. It had always swooped in and taken care of everything with my siblings and parents because I was the oldest. I sincerely believed I had to hold it together all the time. And this heart? It was exhausted from all that effort and, truly, it was on its last beats. For so long, I believed I could be the perfect woman. I could be the perfect mom. I could be the perfect friend, the perfect daughter. But in my heart of hearts, I was at wit's end after the divorce. That's where the wilderness begins.

When you realize your old way of life is no longer sustainable, you find yourself in dire need. Something drastic had to change in my life. And it did. Up to that point, I thought if I wanted to THRIVE, all I had to do was just get divorced! In the wilderness, I realized that God had something else in mind. He wanted me to change my heart and pursue a restored marriage—the opposite of what I'd been telling myself. He gave me the chance to become a Jesus follower and learn to follow him, not just believe in him. That's what getting a new heart is all about.

The dictionary defines the word "THRIVE" this way: to prosper, flourish; be fortunate or successful. We often have our own idea of what this means, but I found out that God has his own definition of what THRIVE means. When God performs a heart transplant, we have a new understanding of what it means to prosper, flourish, and be successful. In our own strength, we don't have the ability to comprehend what God means by THRIVE! And that's why we need someone bigger than us to guide us! God did not need for me to be perfect; he just wanted me to follow him. I could trust him to make a straight path out of the confusion of the wilderness.

I have to point out another tricky thing about timing (that T in THRIVE). You may be wondering why immediately *after* I became a Christian I went straight into the wilderness. Doesn't something about that sound wrong to you? After I decided to follow God, shouldn't I have been divinely airlifted right out of this wilderness mess? Experiencing the wilderness was the absolute last thing I had in mind. I just wanted what I wanted when I wanted it! My perspective of life was very shallow back then; it was all about me and ensuring my comfort. I was initially uninterested in staying in the wilderness one minute longer than I had to! But God would soon show me a better way. Before he could show me *how* he was going to put my marriage back together again, God put me on a path that would develop my ability to persevere and endure. Those two things—perseverance and endurance—are essential to getting through the wilderness. Perseverance is the ability to keep going without knowing where exactly you're going! Endurance is similar, but to me it's an inner strength that develops from perseverance.

R – REMIND MYSELF EACH DAY HOW MUCH GOD LOVES ME

God loves you because he created you! And he created you for his greater purposes, not your own. What if you reminded yourself of these two truths every day? What would change about the way you approach your day?

So many women fumble around in life, not understanding their true purpose and why they are here on Earth. That was me for so long. When you have a clear understanding of how much God loves you, it frees you up to live your life with your hands wide open, following his path for your life, not the path you or anyone else comes up with! It took a while for me to grasp this truth. I had a hard time believing how much God could love me after all I had done. Maybe you can relate.

We wrestle with accepting that God loves us unconditionally. But why would He *not* love you, if he created you for himself and his purposes? If you're finding yourself unable to wrap your arms around this concept, it may be because you have it backwards. It's not about how much (or how little) we love God. It's about how much he loves us, regardless of how we may have failed in the past.

Thriving operates on an eternal perspective of life. It's not about managing to make it through today, tomorrow, or this year. Rather, thriving is that abundant life in John 10:10 that begins now and continues forever in heaven with God. Our life on Earth is not about us. It's about discovering why God has us here in the first place. Let me say it again. It's not about how much we love God, but how much he loves us and even died for us. Life is not about what we do for him.

And, really, what can we "do" for him anyway?

This might be a hard reality check, but God doesn't need you. He definitely wants you to participate in his plan, but he doesn't *need* you to accomplish it. His plan will happen with or without you. Isn't this realization freeing? Isn't this so exhilarating to think we can join God in his work instead of just getting through another day? What an honor to be chosen for this work. How peaceful to know we don't have to perform for him. We just join him where he is already working.

Remember, God chose us, we didn't choose him—yet another concept we get backwards. He created us to fit into his big plan where we get to THRIVE, using the gifts and talents he gave us! We didn't make them up or achieve anything on our own. He lovingly built us a unique way with his own hands—we just have to be self-aware enough to recognize our gifts and nurture them. Start by thinking about how God created you. What are your gifts and talents? Not sure? Go back to the work you did in chapter four and consider again what you are passionate about. What special abilities do you have in this area? Do you know what it means to "nurture" your gifts and talents? How can you do that? Give these questions some thought as you move to the next letter in the THRIVE acronym.

I – BE INTERESTED IN WHAT GOD IS INTERESTED IN

The life lessons behind the first three letters of THRIVE take some time to sink in. Accepting God's Timing, Living with new Hearts, and Reminding ourselves of his love will give us a good foundation to understand the rest of what it means to THRIVE. We must practice these first three foundational truths every day, day after day, in order to move to the next level—the last three letters of THRIVE.

I began to realize that in order for me to THRIVE (here's your I), I must also be Interested in what God is interested in. So many relationships and situations vie for our attention. We are busy! Probably too busy. In order for you to be interested in what God is interested in, you must be curious about him and be willing to participate with him (not work against him). I was interested in a quick fix. God was interested in growing my character.

I have a second "I" to tell you about in the acronym for THRIVE. Being interested in what God is interested in means also being willing to be Interrupted by him. I was going down a treacherous path, destroying my marriage and family with no intention of reuniting during the first two months after the divorce. I was doing my thing and nothing could deter me. By his grace and mercy, God stopped me in my tracks! He "interrupted" me on my path to destruction and pulled me aside to safety.

Interruptions stop you long enough to make you listen. They come in the form of break-ups, illnesses, accidents, crises, crushing blows, and general bad news—they get our attention and we must find out what we're supposed to learn from those circumstances. Interruptions can also involve God's Word speaking loud and clear, which can then change the trajectory of a path we might be going down.

Some of you reading this are curious to try being Interested in what God is interested in. Some of you can see for the first time how God may be Interrupting you to get your attention even now. If that's you, ask Jesus to give you the supernatural desire to know him. Start there. Simply ask him to help you be aware of him throughout your day. Begin to see him at work all around you. Get acquainted with him. That's how I started before I eventually made Jesus the biggest part of my life. One of the most important steps you can take is to open a Bible and study it for yourself to see who he really is. Psalm 34:8 describes someone willing to find out about God like someone trying a new dish for the first time. It reads, "O taste and see that the Lord is good..." Then it switches the description to one that pictures God like a shelter in a storm. We all take refuge somewhere when we're in trouble—but this Psalm pictures someone running to God, maybe for the first time, and declaring how happy he is that he did so.

On the other hand, some of you have been walking with God a long time. You know the Lord and spend time with him every day. Sometimes mature Christians think we have it all figured out—but God can still surprise you. God can still Interrupt you on your path as well. Are you willing to be Interrupted in order to follow his plan, no matter what?

The message behind every Interruption is that we all still have lessons to learn. We may have come a long way spiritually, but there are always areas where we must grow and mature. The key to abundant and purposeful living is to remain teachable and wide open to whatever he has for us. Look at the Interruption in your life as a reminder that God has a greater plan for you. Settle into that fact and take it one day at a time. We grumble and complain because we have an idea of when and how certain things should happen. We impose artificial deadlines on when God should act, but that's just not how it works, is it? We can't rush God, can we? Interruptions and detours on the path of life are confusing and don't make sense in our heads or in our hearts. But remember, God has a plan and his ways are higher and infinitely better than our own.

V – BECOME A VICTOR, NOT A VICTIM

After God interrupted me and my plans for my life, he showed me how to become a conqueror over my chaos. I found inspiration in scriptures like Isaiah 41:10 that says, "Fear not, for I am with you; Be not dismayed, for I am your God; I will strengthen you, I will help you, I will uphold you with my righteous right hand." I also like Isaiah 40:31 because it assures us, "But those who trust in the Lord will renew their strength; They will soar on wings like eagles; They will run and not grow weary; They will walk and not faint." So often we fall into a victim mentality and feel sorry for ourselves. Have you ever noticed that self-focus keeps you, well, self-focused? This mindset can be dangerous in the wilderness. When we play the victim, we never take responsibility for our lives; it's always the fault of something else or someone else. This is not a mentality that can THRIVE. It is, however, a good way to stay lost in the wilderness, wallowing in self-pity. Are you sick yet of being the victim? We must realize that the wilderness tempts us to feel sorry for ourselves.

Experiencing an eating disorder as a young adult for five years was a wilderness experience for me. Waiting for reconciliation with Jeff was wilderness to me. Trying to balance being a stay-at-home mom, but needing to work, was wilderness for me. Being a divorcé was also foreign to me. It was total wilderness. As seven years passed with no resolution to my marriage, I was so tempted to feel like a victim of circumstances. I even briefly contemplated dating when it seemed Jeff and I would never, ever reunite. After Jeff and I married a second time, Lauren's accident happened. That was another wilderness experience for our whole family, as is Jeff's cancer situation right now.

It's what we do with the curve balls, the trials, and the suffering that matters. In the book of James it says in chapter 1:2-4, "Don't run from tests and hardships, brothers and sisters. As difficult as they are, you will ultimately find joy in them; if you embrace them, your faith will blossom under pressure and teach you true patience as you endure. And true patience brought on by endurance will equip you to complete the long journey and cross the finish line—mature, complete, and wanting nothing." (MSG). You can be victorious no matter what comes your way because God is right there walking beside you, even when you think you cannot take another step.

I had to see myself as a Victor in Jesus. A conqueror, nothing less. I could trust and depend on him to come through for me. And because he has the perfect plan for my life, I needed to trust that even if that plan turns out *not* to be what I want it to be, I could trust in that. All I could do was walk forward in victory and do what God was asking me to do—wait, pray, be patient, and see how he was going to bring Jeff and I back together. To my delight I began to see that, even in this wilderness, I could THRIVE.

E – EXPECT GOD TO SHOW UP

Expect God to work, even when you can't see any trace of

him in the wilderness! Wilderness is waiting, remember. So anticipate by faith that he will do what he does best: the supernatural! If you commit to follow him, anticipate that he'll do the impossible and show you a way out of the wilderness. Even if you can't see it today. When God first laid on my heart to pursue reconciliation, I didn't expect much of anything. After several months of learning who God is, I had more faith, but I still did not see him doing much. Years went by with nothing happening. Nada. After five years of waiting for God to restore our marriage, Jeff still did not want to get back together. I had hurt him to the core. Still, I had to believe. So I did. I believed that a God who can do all things could still do something for us.

When God did work his miracle, it was surprising to both of us how many ways he chose to do it. Here is a fun one I remember. A friend of our girls who was ten at the time was spending the night one evening when Jeff and I were still divorced. Out of the blue she blurted out to Jeff at dinner, "Mr. Scruggs, why don't you get back together with Mrs. Scruggs? You love each other more than most married couples I know!" Out of the mouth of babes comes wisdom. God used Erica to speak to truth to Jeff in a big way.

Another time, about the point when I was losing patience with Jeff ever wanting to reconcile, he was in a car accident. He called me from the scene and told me another car had hit him. I got in my car and drove as fast as I could to see him, wondering why it was me he called. Up to that point, Jeff had never done something like that. He never included me in his personal life. The only relationship he'd wanted with me was to parent the girls as best as we could, given the circumstances.

When I arrived at the accident site, Jeff was stunned and shaking, but he didn't have a scratch on him. I nervously slid in the passenger seat beside him. He turned and looked me straight in the eye and said, "I think God is trying to get my attention." That day we decided we would begin dating and develop a new relationship—a thriving relationship with Jesus at the center. But it still took two more years to get to the point where Jeff committed to remarrying.

SEASONS OF THE WILDERNESS

Jeff and I have been remarried over 20 years now. Our family has since endured many more wilderness experiences together. Some journeys were brief; and some were intense, including Lauren's accident. When you're looking at Christmas lights one moment and the next moment you're in intensive care thinking your daughter might not survive her injuries, suddenly you're in the wilderness again.

About three years ago, I felt as if God were telling me, "Cheryl, I'm shifting things." I didn't know what that meant, but it was an impression I had on my heart. Jeff and I were in our sixties, which is a shifting experience in itself. It's a milestone. You're looking back on all you've accomplished and charting toward what's ahead. I told Jeff what I thought God was saying, but for three years nothing major happened. Then Jeff got cancer. We did not see that coming, to say the least, since we are health nuts and clean eaters who are committed to staying in shape and doing all things healthy. We teach others about healthy living, so this diagnosis blew us away. It rocked my world as a woman and a wife.

Suddenly, here we are in the wilderness again. But just

because we're in a place of struggle doesn't mean we can't THRIVE. You can THRIVE in difficulty without necessarily *feeling* as if you're thriving. Let me explain. Thriving is learning to be okay with feeling sad, angry, and lost as you process what's happening. Remember, living abundantly doesn't depend on your circumstances. And you're learning that thriving is learning to accept and deal with what's going on inside of you. God created a range of human emotions, right? Where people get stuck is thinking they can't THRIVE because they're waiting to feel better. Or they're waiting to meet someone new after a breakup. Or they're unemployed and waiting to get hired. Once that happens, they say, *then* they will thrive.

That's a lot of waiting.

Instead of thinking we're not thriving because the thing we want hasn't happened yet, let me ask you something. Can we contemplate and look deeper into ourselves as we recover from those moments and ask what we're supposed to learn? *What part am I playing? What part do others play? What am I learning?* You don't find a 1-2-3 list of things to "do" in the wilderness. A lot of times there's nothing to do—you're waiting, remember? In the waiting, you instead learn a new way to "be." The way you'll know that you were thriving all along is when you look back one day and realize how much you grew as a person because of the wilderness. You wouldn't trade what you learned and who you became for anything.

PRACTICING THE LOST ARTS OF BEING HUMAN

I'm always looking for what God is trying to teach me, but that doesn't mean that I don't wonder, "Why is this so hard? Why me? Why our family?" More than anything, I want to be grounded every day because I never know when I'll find myself in the wilderness again. The following Lost Arts are ones I think will help you while you're waiting in the wilderness. Has it been a long time since you practiced heartfelt gratitude? Are you skilled at living in the moment instead of charting ahead?

THE LOST ART OF GRATITUDE

One of the most difficult things to accomplish is being truly grateful in the hard times. As a whole, people are generally not practicing gratitude. In the wilderness, gratitude is a rarity because we're focused on what we *don't* have. We *don't* have answers. We *don't* have what we think we need. We *don't* have a plan. But look around—what do you have that you can be grateful for? It requires the same skill of paying attention to what matters. Write a thank you note to a friend. Call a family member you appreciate and tell him or her so. Now is a time when we need to care for each other more than ever. Expressing gratitude is really a way of serving someone. It encourages them. It lifts them up. Expressing gratitude to God is a way to keep us humble and recognize all he has given us.

Those who are not grateful in their approach to life tend to be miserable. They are unhappy because they perceive they never have enough—even if they have much more than you and I have combined! This misconception has nothing to do with the size of people's bank accounts. There is an ache in the heart of all ungrateful people, and they don't know what it is. Do you feel unsettled, steeped in self-pity? Are you often vaguely frustrated or grumpy? These are all symptoms of ingratitude. In contrast, when you are practicing gratitude on a regular basis, you are not as self-focused and needy.

Questions to ask about gratitude:

What are you grateful for in this moment?

Have you ever made a "grateful list"? Try using the categories from this book and name what you are grateful for spiritually, emotionally, relationally, physically, and mentally.

THE LOST ART OF SAVORING THE MOMENT

Part of the frustration of the wilderness is the unsatisfied desire to chart ahead and figure out where the path is leading. We often don't have much to go on in the wilderness. Time slows and we just drift through the day. We feel stuck in a place we don't like and life seems to be passing us by.

Knowing that God has placed us exactly where we are—even in the wilderness—is a refreshing perspective. He has a purpose for you, even though you can't see that right now. Stop charting ahead and start noticing the little moments today. Life doesn't start when you get out of the wilderness; it's happening all along. My fear for you is that you're missing life right in front of you if you insist on figuring out your entire future before you can be happy. And remember, it is contentment and joy we are after, not fleeting happiness.

To "savor" means to enjoy something completely. Let me get you started with some ideas.

Make a new practice of savoring the moment in the early mornings or late evenings with some routines to help you slow down before you rush off into your day and allow you to wind down and reflect when the day is over. For example, at the start of your day, get up early and be quiet for the first few minutes. (This may mean getting up before anyone else in the house is awake!) Keep the distractions to a minimum. No morning news. Hold off on the social media scrolling. Just find a comfortable chair and write in your journal about the day ahead. Read some scripture. Take a moment to pray. At the end of the day, take a quick walk to decompress. Maybe take a hot bath or shower to relax. Pour a glass of wine. Call a friend. Listen to your favorite playlist. What savor-the-moment routines could you build into your mornings and evenings that appeal to you?

Savoring can also start in the kitchen. Cooking and baking create aromas that make people who walk in your home wonder, "What is she making?" Roasted potatoes are my go-to when I want to create a lovely aroma in my kitchen that I know will please my family and guests. It's nothing but potatoes, rosemary, garlic, salt and pepper, and olive oil, but it works wonders to help others savor the moment, too.

Go outside. Tending to plants and watching them thrive and grow is another way to force yourself to be present and savor a small moment outdoors. Or go for a walk around your neighborhood. Take notice of your surroundings. Engage your senses—what can you see, taste, smell, hear, touch? Pay attention to what you're tasting when you're eating. Can you taste salt, sweet, sour in an individual bite? What is the texture? Try to describe it. Mindless eating is the opposite of savoring.

Conversation is another savor point. When others are talking, sit back, and savor the moment. You're with loved ones. This is the good stuff. Does your husband look tired while he's talking? Is your teenager troubled? Does your family seem joyful? Can you tell when friends have something on their mind? Pay attention and cherish your time with the people you love.

We do so much of life without noticing. Savoring takes life to the next level. We have one life to live. That's it. And I don't have to remind you that if we don't savor the moments that are passing us by, one day we'll want those moments back.

Questions to ask about savoring the moment:

There are a million moments in a day. What are you paying attention to as a day opens up each morning?

What do you notice? Look around—what are the sounds and smells?

When the day is over, what routines help you pay attention and reflect on the day?

Look around you again at the end of the day. What conversations take place? What's everyone's demeanor—and what are your own feelings, emotions, and thoughts?

How can you better savor your time with others? What is worth noticing?

How is busyness keeping you from having the time to savor the moment?

CHAPTER SEVEN

HAZARDS OF FEAR-BASED LIVING

I'M NO DAREDEVIL. SNOW SKI? YES, BUT I DON'T LIKE to go fast. In fact, leave me in the lodge with coffee and a good book instead. Jeff went skydiving one time with a Navy Seals friend, but that is the last thing I'm ever going to do. Maybe if there was big money attached to it, but even then, there's probably no way I'm getting in that plane.

The truth is, we're all more afraid of certain people and situations than ski lifts and skydiving. We're nervous and scared of what people think of us to varying degrees. We're apprehensive about the possibility of failure. We dread being embarrassed and avoid it at all costs. All of this fear-based living affects our behavior and keeps us from thriving.

Don't believe your life is controlled by fear? Let's find

out. Read the following statements and choose a number between 1-5 that best describes you.

1 – **Not true of me**

2 – **Rarely true of me**

3 – **Somewhat true of me**

4 – **Often true of me**

5 – **Very true of me**

____ I have a hard time saying "no" to others.

____ I'm always open to trying something new.

____ I often over-commit myself.

____ What others think is very important to me.

____ I often seek multiple opinions before I make a decision.

____ Worry never wakes me up at night.

____ I rarely re-hash difficult conversations in my mind.

____ I feel angry much of the time—even if I don't show it.

In my fifties, I learned just how much of my everyday behavior was driven by fear. I was stunned! I consider myself a confident woman. But we only have so much energy, and mine was being unwittingly zapped by fears I didn't realize I had. Where are you burning more fuel than you need to physically, emotionally, mentally, relationally, and spiritually every week? Are you over-committing yourself because you don't want to tell someone "no"? Do you spend inordinate energy on maintaining your looks, your status, your home, and material possessions—all for someone else's approval? Do you spend a lot of time seeking spiritual things like attending church, reading the Bible, or going to a Bible study solely to make sure others think you're "spiritual enough"? How often do you wake up worried or operate during the day off a baseline of stress?

I live in Dallas where outward appearance is important. You've at least seen commercials for *Real Housewives*, right? Sure, I fix my hair and love to put a little color on my face to feel bright and cheery, but if I'm running up the street to meet Jeff for lunch, I'm not taking two hours to get ready. I don't care if I see anyone there, and we see people we know quite frequently when we're out. Women for whom appearance is everything live in mortal fear of moments like that. They get so bogged down that they miss the good stuff of having lunch. They miss conversations. They miss meeting someone new or developing a relationship that needs to grow. They are that afraid of what others might think if they're not measuring up to some standard.

I remember going to Bible study one season at a church where perfectly coifed women seemed more petrified of each other, rather than attending a Bible study to learn something about God. Fear got in the way of what they wanted to do in the first place—learn about the Bible! "This is nuts. I can't do this," I remember thinking on the way home. That environment would fire up instinctive fears in most women. And that is not me.

ANGER STEMS FROM FEAR

I had a ton of anger after my divorce. "Anger is the fluid love bleeds when it is cut," a theologian named C.S. Lewis once said. My anger had to do with the fear of being rejected by the man I loved and him seeing me as something less than perfect. As I've said, I didn't open up with Jeff about my feelings before our divorce because I feared he would no longer see me as perfect. He was on a pedestal of my own making; I put him there. But I resented feeling as though I was missing the mark in comparison to him. Stuffing emotions inside of me eventually came to a full boil. The reality is that I started to get angry in year two of the marriage, but we didn't divorce until 10 years into our marriage. So for nine years I was terrified of telling Jeff I wasn't happy or that something in our marriage did not feel right. I just kept everything to myself year after year, while resentment simmered and boiled inside. I've since experienced two one-year stints of counseling and read many books to deal with negative emotions. Along the way, I found something that my resentment, bitterness, and anger all had in common. Tracing these emotions back to the root of fear was helpful to my understanding where they were coming from.

FEAR COMPLICATES LIFE

Fear is contrary to thriving. Thriving is an easy flow. But fear complicates and affects your life in a myriad of ways you may not be aware of. My experience as a Biblical marriage counselor has proven to me time and again how often fear shows up in our lives and strangles our ability to live an abundant, free life. Ironically, most people don't think they're afraid. They do not believe much of their life is controlled by fear at all. People readily say they're "afraid" of spiders or public speaking, and that may be true, but the truth goes much deeper than that. Do we fear what others think of us? Are we afraid to be our true selves? Do we refuse to try a new career or take a new path because we are afraid of public ridicule and failure? We all have fear-based saboteurs at work inside us—certain attitudes and thought patterns that hold us back and sometimes hold us hostage. They keep us from becoming the person we're meant to be and reaching our full potential.

I don't mind confessing that I still struggle with fear-based living, despite how much progress I've made. Fear complicates some of my relationships with others, for example. When I'm hurt, I shut down emotionally. I'll get passive aggressive and not make eye contact with the person or just shun them. I'm super embarrassed about this behavior, which shows just how much I am a work in progress! This knee-jerk reaction is not something I'm proud of—and it's not what I want to do. But still, it happens.

Being passive aggressive is a characteristic of fear-based living. Did you know that? This is how it works. You feel angry, but you're afraid of how it will be received if you express why you're angry, so you turn passive aggressive and use sarcasm and subtle digs. You might even completely shut down and not talk. For me, I go radio silent usually because I'm afraid to express my anger or frustration. I end up not saying anything and act aloof. Most often, the root of passive aggressive behavior is being afraid of not being loved or approved of. Or you're afraid of coming across as dumb and being shunned if you speak up for yourself, so your defense is passive aggressiveness. This reaction always makes things worse.

Through lots of counseling, I've discovered why this occurs in my life and the generational trauma that goes with it. But my goal, and where I continue to make progress, is being aware and doing something about it. My ultimate goal is freedom. My deep desire is to have and maintain the most amazing relationships with others. I want to be the best I can be, not only because God wants me to do so but also in order to be the best "me" for the benefit of others.

Don't let anyone fool you. We all have wounds and dysfunction in our lives that operate every single day within us, but pride makes us think it's the other person who's the problem! The Bible says, "Do not judge *and* criticize *and* condemn [others unfairly with an attitude of self-righteous superiority as though assuming the office of a judge], so that you will not be judged [unfairly]. For just as you [hypocritically] judge others [when you are sinful and unrepentant], so will you be judged; and in accordance with your standard of measure [used to pass out judgment], judgment will be measured to you. Why do you look at the [insignificant] speck that is in your brother's eye, but do not notice *and* acknowledge the [egregious] log that is in your own eye?" Matthew 7:1-5 (AMP).

I can't judge the other person; I have to examine myself and ask the hard questions. What am I afraid of? Being re-hurt? If you want to thrive, you need to process and think about why you react a certain way in some situations and in certain relationships—and put a name on the saboteurs that are keeping you in fear. A saboteur is something that makes you act out of your negative, unhealthy, sinful, and insecure self.

FEAR AND SELF-SABOTAGE

You can take personality tests to find out more about your specific saboteurs. For example, I'm in a leadership group that often utilizes the insights from a mental health organization at www.PositiveIntelligence.com. When I took their test online, it revealed that my top two "saboteurs" are being hyper-vigilant and controlling, a throwback to my childhood.

I feel nervous whenever I'm not in control, which fans the flame and creates the notion that I have to be even more vigilant. Both of these negative behaviors—hyper-vigilance and control—are based in fear. Few people know that I have a shy side. I don't mind that part of me, but I don't want to live like that. Certain social situations tap into an old fear that I'm not going to be approved of for some reason. Then I tend to get nervous and "think out loud" while talking. That's not always healthy because I interrupt and/or blurt out things I don't even mean! From there, it's a quick spiral down to feeling misunderstood, and on it goes. Yuck! It's my way of processing, but this is not the way to do it. In my healthy relationships, I can do this without facing judgment because the other person has taken time to know me, my weaknesses, and my faults. What I love most is that these safe people offer me grace and encouragement—and I do the same for them. What a gift!

Here's another example of fear-based living from the pages of my life. If I sense someone has unrealistic expectations of me and there's the strong possibility that I'll disappoint them, that's super scary to me. I turn inward and grow quiet. I don't feel like myself in those situations, and I get flustered.

I am working hard at reeling back all these saboteurs complicating my relationships. I am trying to be more cognizant of how and when those fears are at work. To ease your mind, this is a lifelong journey we're all on, and we will never "arrive"! A war rages back and forth our whole lives between our healthy self and our unhealthy self. Of course, we don't always sit around wondering, "Am I living out of my healthy self or my unhealthy self?" But this practice is actually beneficial to do on a regular basis, so it's worth learning the value of doing so. Start with realizing that you have both versions of yourself operating throughout the day. Be intrigued by that dichotomy. Start to name some of your saboteurs so you can deal with them.

Unhealthy is being restless and afraid, in constant fight or flight mode. Healthy is being able to deal with what happens on an even keel. The goal is to live out your healthy, abundant self—the one God made you to be. Let me give an example of living out of my healthy self. When someone or something taps into my insecurities and fears, and I react calmly—that's my healthy self doing the talking. It's as if God gives me the words to say. I feel calm, confident, and secure. At that moment, I am not anxious, hypervigilant, defensive, or insecure—walking around with a dull stomachache. I feel like myself: my healthy, God-given self. I experience peace and have lots of joy. When I'm slow to speak and quick to give grace from my best self, I'm more like the person God made me to be.

I also don't allow another person's insecurities or dysfunction to interrupt my healthy self. That is in their court. That is theirs to figure out. We must be aware when co-dependency tries to take over and leaves us feeling responsible for another person's problems to an unhealthy degree. Co-dependency leads us to think, "If you're happy, then I'm happy." Or "If you're sad, I have to be sad." Ten years ago, I felt overly responsible for people's problems, offering advice without being asked and taking on their issues as my own. I'm not there yet, but I'm way more healed in these areas today because I continue to do the hard work of living out my healthiest self. Please know, sometimes we are mentally or physically spent, and living out our healthiest self can seem daunting and impossible. But the goal is to stay tethered to Jesus and allow him to fill you, help you, and sometimes even carry you.

FEAR AND GENERATIONAL TRAUMA

We all have hurts and habits and traumas and pain from our growing up years. We all have stories. The reason why is because no one is the perfect parent—and no one had the perfect parents. Identifying the negative trends in your family helps you understand that generational trauma is real. And it affects each person in the family in a different way. It's not something to be obsessed about, thinking and filtering everything constantly. We can also take this too far. But doing the hard work to understand your family of origin is very freeing!

For example, maybe your dad had an alcoholic father; maybe your grandmother had mental illness. These super unhealthy trends develop fear-based habits and behavior that filter down and play a part in our lives, like it or not. I don't know your father. But I know that he was affected by how his father treated him, which affected how he treated you. If his dad was healthy, he learned from a healthy example and hopefully chose to pass this healthy trend down to you. If his dad had a raging temper, one of two things happened. Either your dad dealt with the fear and pain and decided he would never put his family through something like that. Or his father's temper negatively affected your dad's relationships with you. We can address this stuff and halt the generational trauma, or it passes on to varying degrees to the next generation. What did you miss out on in your childhood? Do you have anger toward anyone in your family? What about your childhood is hard to remember?

In my experience, I've noticed people are mostly living in the present without a thought to the generational traumas from their past. They're just not going back and seeing what's there because they don't want to put in the effort. They're content to live out their unhealthiness. But that's not you, thriver. And it's not me either! We're on a different path than the rest of the world because we've decided we're not going to live out the unhealthy part of ourselves anymore. My unhealthy self most likely comes from trauma in my past. I know that. So I want to help others unpack their generational traumas too.

Thriving is not just a decision you make for you—it's also for those you love because you don't want to pass on the negative parts of your past that affect you today. Whatever knee-jerk behavior makes you feel juvenile and embarrassed, but you just can't help yourself, needs to be dealt with. I'm my children's mother and my grandchildren's grandmother—I owe it to them to be at my healthiest emotionally. That truth has hit me hard lately. If I see something I don't want in my behavior, thankfully I can do something about it. I'm not a victim. I can pray and work on changing myself. You can ask your family to pray for you, that the generational curse from your past will be gone from you. That's powerful. The decision boils down to: Do I really want to thrive and what am I going to do to get there?

WORRY FUELS OUR WORST FEARS

Anxiety is the cornerstone of fear-based living. The longer we worry, the more likely our anxiety will turn into paralyzing fear of the unknown. Think about what you learned about the wilderness experience in the last chapter. Worry has the opportunity to turn into fear over time, the longer we're in the wilderness. The Hebrews' journey to the Promised Land was 40 years!

There's so much I love in this ancient story of men and women who had to remember that God was with them, leading them. When they finally got to their destination, God had to instruct them how to live in this new and unknown place where they knew no one and nothing. Talk about anxiety and worry! Look at the first verse in this long passage from Deuteronomy 8 that describes the scene. In this moment God says to obey the commands he gave them "today..." In other words, he instructs them just to take it one day at a time.

> The whole commandment that I command you today you shall be careful to do, that you may live and multiply, and go in and possess the land that the Lord swore to give to your fathers. [2] And you shall *remember the whole way that the Lord your God has led you these forty years in the wilderness,*

> that he might humble you, testing you to know what was in your heart, whether you would keep his commandments or not. [3] And he humbled you and let you hunger and fed you with manna, which you did not know, nor did your fathers know, that he might make you know that man does not live by bread alone, but man lives by every word that comes from the mouth of the Lord. [4] Your clothing did not wear out on you and your foot did not swell these forty years. [5] Know then in your heart that, as a man disciplines his son, the Lord your God disciplines you. [6] So you shall keep the commandments of the Lord your God by walking in his ways and by fearing him. [7] *For the Lord your God is bringing you into a good land, a land of brooks of water, of fountains and springs, flowing out in the valleys and hills,* [8] *a land of wheat and barley, of vines and fig trees and pomegranates, a land of olive trees and honey,* [9] *a land in which you will eat bread without scarcity, in which you will lack nothing, a land whose stones are iron, and out of whose hills you can dig copper.* [10] *And you shall eat and be full, and you shall bless the Lord your God for the good land he has given you.* Deuteronomy 8:1-10

You can't look ahead or down the road very far without being afraid of the future, especially in this day and age. So just focus on this day, this single day. That's the advice God gave the Hebrews and it's still pertinent for us today. Jesus also said not to worry about tomorrow because "each day has enough trouble of its own." Most wilderness experiences are not over in a week or two. It takes time to get over heartache when someone leaves you, for example. Getting through a cancer diagnosis is certainly not something that takes a few months and you're done. You have to take these anxiety-ridden situations one day at a time. What God has taught me time and again during my wilderness periods is how to endure and persevere *with him*! Not just endure and persevere, but *with him*. We never know what he is trying to teach us or show us. And we certainly don't know his plan. If we can trust that the wilderness can show us God's plan, then bring it on!

And notice that verse two indicates part of the reason why God allows these worry-filled situations to flood our lives. The Hebrews wandered around for 40 years in the desert wilderness of the Middle East. Why? God says in this passage that he wanted to "test" their hearts. He wants to see (and show you) where your heart is in the wilderness. I have a good idea where your heart will be. It will likely be broken and fearful. Life is not happiness all the time. That's just not what thriving means. Thriving sometimes means resting in the painful seasons and not giving up. That's all that is required to make it.

But we must realize that there is also the possibility for joy in the wilderness. It sounds counter-intuitive, but joy arises from the ashes of suffering many times because we grow so much during the hard times. And we can be joyful knowing that this pain is for a season. For example, being a single mom wasn't something I anticipated happening, but it was a very joyful time for me to pour into my kids emotionally and spiritually. When they were in elementary school, I hosted a small Bible study at my house with their friends, some of whom remain best friends to this day. Just the other day some of these friends were reminiscing with me about the homemade pizza I served every Sunday. I'm proud of that joy-filled memory in the midst of everything that was going on at that time!

The joy I experienced in the wilderness of waiting for reconciliation with Jeff is that I never felt pressure as a single mom. It was a challenge, but I never thought I was unable to manage it. I loved raising my kids and didn't feel overwhelmed at all, except for providing for them financially.

We can experience joy knowing that God is bringing us to something better eventually. I want you to see in this passage the wonderful description of where he was taking the Hebrews. The Promised Land was a "good" land chock-full of blessings, beyond their imagination. Back in the day when I first read this passage, I knew right away that the "land" for me was a new marriage with Jeff. The land was my chance for a do-over to do it God's way. God eventually brought me to that land—and it was everything I wanted and more.

For you, "the land" is whatever thriving looks like for you. The land is something different all the time. That's why we've spent so much time in this book painting a picture of how you want your life to be in specific areas. Think of it as a place with rushing brooks of clear water, vibrant trees and plants, and lush green pastures. In contrast, the wilderness is a wild and uncultivated desert. It's an uninhabitable, barren place of fear-based living. The "land" symbolizes being brought to some point, condition, or state in life where you can joyfully thrive fear-free. That's where you're meant to be.

RELATIONSHIPS HELP YOU DEAL WITH FEARS

Fear-based living is not something you shake yourself free from—you need others who will help you get past whatever it is you're afraid of in your relationships and circumstances. For example, I thought about writing this book for five years before I published it. Finally, my good friends who are also published encouraged me to quit thinking about it and put something down on paper. I needed that nudge in the right direction to get over my fear that no one would buy the book. Our natural tendency is to procrastinate and avoid. You'll know you are no longer controlled by fear when you take action and do something about it.

I'm especially fond of relationships with older generations of people who can speak into our lives and help us with this. No matter what age you are, you can benefit from the stories of older men and women who know a thing or two about dealing with worry, anxiety, and fear. You're never too old to find someone older and wiser. I have a handful of older people I love spending time with. My Aunt Eva, who is also my godmother, is a very wise woman. She's now in her eighties and calls me often. In fact, she has many women across the United States whom she regularly calls just to touch base and encourage them. In many ways, Eva is a role model for me. I only see her every few years, but I know I can rely on her to be there for me (and me for her) spiritually and emotionally. Who are your heroes or role models who can help you when you're struggling? Pay attention to the people you seek wisdom from. And if you're not seeking wiser, older perspectives that are far outside the easy reach of your own immediate peer group, why not?

You could learn a lot.

And you have a lot to give older people in return. Don't just garner their wisdom—develop a mutual relationship and friendship. You have a lot of love to give as well as gain in friendships with older generations. I've really enjoyed time with my Uncle Bob who is now 96 years old. A veteran of the Korean War, he was full of stories. I will never forget hearing about the day he and his men were crouching in the trenches, exhausted and starving after many nights of fighting. They had one little can of peaches left in their rations. He said they must have passed that aluminum can around to about 20 soldiers, each man taking a small, selfless bite of a piece of peach until the container was empty.

Uncle Bob played a significant role in helping us when Lauren was injured. Lauren lost her eye and hand in the accident, and he spent time with her, sharing wisdom from his experiences. He was shot several times during battle and still has metal shrapnel in his legs. His stories about the resilience of the human spirit and what it takes to keep moving forward after suffering inspired all of us during a time when we all felt lost.

How this opportunity came about was sort of funny. Lauren was hurt in December, and Uncle Bob told us early in the New Year that he would be traveling to Texas to spend time with her, but he didn't set a date. He never answered his phone to follow up, and we weren't quite sure when he was coming to Texas. One afternoon in April, completely unannounced, he just showed up! We sat at our kitchen table for hours, listening with rapt attention to all he had to say and every nugget of wisdom he shared. What a huge memory for me—not only did he show up at our house, but he also showed up for my daughter in a big way. It wasn't the first time he had done that for our family. When my father died, I remember my rough-hewn, war veteran uncle's sudden tears and the tender way he touched my dad's casket and whispered, "I'll miss you buddy."

When we connect with older generations for wisdom, we're treated to stories. We have a lot to learn from other people's stories. That's the interchange we need more of today. Who knows? Maybe you can help someone else get past their own fears. Your life experiences comprise a rich source of wisdom that you can share with younger generations who need to hear those stories—the things you did right and your regrets.

You need wisdom to speak to your fears; winging it in the wilderness won't do. When you are beside yourself with worries and anxiety about the world you suddenly find yourself in, ask those who have been in this world longer than you have. Sage women and men in our lives are not giving the answers to life's tests; they're just strengthening and encouraging generations coming after them.

PRACTICING THE LOST ARTS OF BEING HUMAN

THE LOST ART OF PLAY AND LAUGHTER

I looked up the definition of "laughter" and it read: "glee, hilarity, rejoicing." We all need a big dose of this in our lives. Play and laughter are definitely lost arts because they're in such low supply in society today. We talk about being the grown-ups in the room. How long has it been since you let yourself be playful? When was the last time you didn't take yourself or your life so seriously and, instead, pursued a game or activity with family and friends where you let your hair down?

My saboteurs of being hyper-vigilant and controlling only come out when someone or something ruffles me and I react with these two fear-based characteristics. But my deep self, my real self, is fun and loving. That's who I am and who I want to be. How far away play and laughter can be when we take ourselves too seriously. When you're judging yourself (which we do a lot of, whether we admit it or not), you're on the sidelines. You're not out there on the field playing and enjoying life.

Questions about play and laughter:

What do you like to do for fun? What does "playing" look like for you? What do you enjoy for recreation?

Do you remember the last time you thought about your favorite pastime?

What and who makes you laugh hard?

What do you like to do for entertainment?

What do you do to relax?

THE LOST ART OF COURAGE

Back in 2016 I knew I was supposed to be expanding my reach to women. I wanted to write a blog about all I was learning. But blogs were a dime a dozen back then. My girls challenged me to host a podcast instead. A podcast? I had never done something like that. What if it bombs? What if no one wants to be on my podcast? What if no one listens? Fears popped up at every turn.

But I owe it to my daughters for giving me the courage to give it a try. I spent six months researching how to have a successful podcast, and nine months later I recorded my first episode. Hundreds of episodes later, the podcast is something I look forward to every week. Without my girls, I never would have thought of hosting a podcast, much less gotten over my fear of failure.

Questions to ask about courage:

Do you consider yourself brave? Why or why not?

What does "being brave" mean to you? Think of an example.

When you have a challenge in front of you and feel scared, what is your typical response? Muster up courage to take it on? Or shrink back and say forget it, it's too hard?

Can you face difficulty, pain, or danger without fear?

Are you courageous enough to stand up for your beliefs?

THE LOST ART OF READING TO LEARN

Fear is something you'll have to unpack in your life. What helped me deal with fear is reading books about dealing with the emotional and mental fears I know I have. The problem is that reading to learn is also a Lost Art today! Are you willing to contemplate what you're reading and learning in your free time, or are you just kind of flipping through short quotes and bits and pieces? How often we catch ourselves skimming and reading in snatches while allowing no time for contemplation.

People don't read as much in our culture today. It's definitely a Lost Art that generations before us used to practice much more often when there was no competition from our televisions and phones. We've been trained by marketing experts over many decades to digest information in 30-second commercials and sound bites. When Instagram first became popular, the trend was for people to post several paragraphs about a topic or viewpoint. People *can't* read that much anymore. A social media expert advised me to condense my posts to two or three short sentences. Max. I was intrigued to read about studies showing people can only listen to podcasts that are less than 30 minutes, not an hour or more, even if it's interesting. That's why my Thriving Beyond Belief podcast episodes are only 30 minutes.

When I say that I sometimes sit and read two hours at a time, I know that catches some people off guard. They think they'd have to get up at three in the morning to have the luxury of that kind of time. I have way more time than my thirty-something daughters who are busy raising kids. They get up early and run the whole day with their little ones.

When I was visiting one of my daughters and telling her about the focus of this book, she commented, "Oh my gosh, Mom. A lot of young people don't read anymore." But then to my surprise she added, "But you know what? I think it's coming back." She educated me that afternoon about the trends surrounding twenty- and thirty-somethings posting online about the hardback books they're reading. Younger generations are getting back to something as traditional as reading a book. And they're often doing so because they're figuring out the shortcomings of living a shallow Twitterverse life and feeling really empty. How can someone who has it all be empty? How can they possibly struggle in their marriages? It can and does happen because we're human—and our failures and struggles are the common denominators linking us all. Extraordinarily successful people can do whatever they want financially, but even many of them admit to feeling a void spiritually and emotionally. People are reaching out and wanting to nurture themselves in new (and old) ways—and many are making the time to do so by reading.

When I talk about nurturing the skill of reading and how it ties in with the idea of thriving, I often encounter questions. What about fiction? While I think you'll get more out of reading to learn something, there is certainly space for reading fiction and just letting your mind shift into neutral. A fiction book may have lots of teaching points, but sometimes just reading a good story can teach you how to have fun and relax!

What about audio books and podcasts? Absolutely! Not everyone reads. You can get a relatively inexpensive subscription to listen to audio books or rent them from your local library. Many of the Lost Arts lock arms and work together to improve our lives and deliver us from fears and bad habits we've learned in a modern age. Fear debilitates. Intentionally plugging into more resting, thinking, and reading makes a big difference in our mental, emotional, and spiritual health.

Questions to ask about reading to learn:

Why do you like to read? If you're "not a reader," why not?

What is scary or intimidating about learning new things?

Would others describe you as being curious? Would they describe you as a lifelong learner? Why or why not?

Think of some person, place, or thing you want to learn more about. What topics really excite or really bore you?

CHAPTER EIGHT

THRIVING IN COMMUNITY

DURING THE COVID LOCKDOWNS, LONELINESS HIT a fever pitch in our nation and throughout the world. We see how extremely lonely and isolated people are today and many assume it's because of the pandemic. However, I have a different take because the loneliness factor was already playing a significant and alarming role in our culture long before lockdowns set in. We couldn't be with our friends during the lockdowns, and that made us acutely aware of our emptiness. But I suspect that we were already excruciatingly lonely in the deepest parts of who we are, having spent many *years* before Covid without cultivating satisfying, intimate, thriving friendships and relationships with loved ones.

If we're honest, many of us have experienced a lifetime of general apathy and continual busyness that keeps us from getting to know others on a deep and mutually enriching level. There's something eye-opening about that realization. Even when we are regularly with our friends in social settings, we don't necessarily feel any closer afterward. But that can change, and it must if we want to enjoy life to the full. Here's the big question: What are you doing right now to help your most important relationships thrive for the rest of your life? Don't worry if you're stumped. Throughout this chapter, I'm going to challenge you so you'll know exactly how to answer that question. I'll show you some practical habits to implement right away to build and sustain a healthy community that yields a lifetime of benefits.

WHAT IS COMMUNITY?

"Community" is sometimes an overused buzz word. I'm naturally rebellious and don't want to write what's already been said by many authors and experts about our need for community. Instead, let's go deeper than that, even at the risk of stepping on some toes. If you are at the beginning stages of learning to thrive, I've included this chapter on community because I want you to know that you are not embarking on this journey alone. There are many women asking themselves the same hard questions about how they want to invest their remaining time, whether it's long or short. Everyone struggles. Every family has trouble with kids, marriage issues, and financial hardships—but you wouldn't necessarily know it because we keep those parts of ourselves to ourselves. People also struggle with feeling disconnected spiritually. Or they lack emotional connection in certain relationships. Or they aren't physically where they would like to be. In general, people are willing to be part of community of others, but they are not so willing to talk in a meaningful, revealing way about this kind of stuff. Why is that?

I host several virtual groups of women online that started during the pandemic and continue to this day. One day a member of a group broke down crying. She'd never done that before in our group and told me later that she was struggling with some serious problems in her family. I was taken aback. We'd been meeting for many months, and I had no idea what she had been going through. No one did. When I asked her why she had never confided in the group before, she admitted, "Oh, I could never share something personal like that with the group..." She was willing to meet with women weekly, but being vulnerable and talking about what really mattered in her life was another matter.

Like her, we're craving deeper conversations and connections, but we don't know how to bring them about in real life. There are groups of women who have been getting together for golf, girls night out, lunch, and dinner for months and even years—and know nothing meaningful about each other. That's not thriving, but this is the story of every community throughout America. There is so much going on behind closed doors that women feel they cannot talk about for fear of being judged and ostracized—even at church. And one of the biggest deterrents is feeling insecure, shameful, or guilty about their circumstances.

Instead, I advocate not only a new way of thinking and relating to the world around you, but also supply the practical skills and tools to put these skills into practice. If it doesn't work or apply in real life, it's not helpful. One of the most practical skills I can offer you to help you develop more authentic community in your life is to build your courage and start initiating and experiencing conversations that matter, and this begins with listening.

PRACTICE ACTIVE LISTENING

This is another key area for you to evaluate your current level of community. Are you sometimes accused of appearing to "not listen" to your friends or family? Are you truly interested in what another person has to say, or do you just tolerate a conversation to appear "nice"? If these questions hit a nerve, you may benefit from practicing active listening skills. Active listening is more than just hearing what the other person said and regurgitating content. When someone is sitting across from you at the coffee shop and asks, "Hey, are you listening to me?" it's tempting to fake it if you haven't been listening! Some people parrot back the words without the *meaning*. That's not listening. That's regurgitating.

On the other hand, active listening entails hearing and interpreting the meaning behind the words the other person is using. Being socially aware means that you're on my radar, and I'm not so concerned that I get my point across in every conversation with you. Remember, try to understand, rather than be understood. The dictionary definition of "aware" also includes being "sophisticated" in our approach to others and being "informed." Are you mindful enough of others to ask meaningful follow-up questions in the process of listening to someone? You know people better when you ask questions and are aware of what they're saying and what they mean. Going deeper in conversation with someone will train you to listen for greater meanings.

Here are some tips for active listening:

- Make eye contact with the person with whom we're talking. This alone can do wonders for our ability to understand someone better.
- Break the habit of assuming we know what the other person is saying. Ask follow up questions. Clarify. Hear what others are truly saying first before you respond.
- Don't just wait and silently focus on what you're going to say next—remain in the moment.
- Pay attention to how the conversation is going. Is it flowing easily? That's a good sign you're engaged and participating.
- Look for opportunities to exert positive influence on someone else, especially if this is a mentoring relationship where you are the mentor and someone is looking to you for advice.

Listening essentially equals paying attention, something we went into detail about earlier. All the skills you're learning as you thrive will overlap at many points. Try to practice active listening today, and pay attention to your listening. Afterward, ask yourself how you did. What did you hear? What was your body language while listening? What was different about the conversation? We listen in order to make note of something. The more we listen, the deeper our listening goes. You'll be surprised how much your listening helps others talk and reveal themselves more to you. You create a safe space for them to be themselves when you listen. You'll deepen your relationships with others and incorporate more emotional intimacy, which will enrich your sense of community in ways you can only imagine.

HONORING SOMEONE VS. CROSSING A LINE

Practicing the Lost Arts of Being Human, listening, and paying attention, can help you know yourself and others better. And don't forget that these are called "Lost Arts" because we all lost sight of them somewhere along the way. Practicing them is about recovering and reclaiming what's been lost. The "lost part" of developing close relationships is that, as a culture, we started being afraid of asking intimate questions instead of blessing someone with our interest in their lives. We started isolating in our own little worlds, turning inward, and making excuses for rarely scratching the surface of the wonderfully complex design of others and finding out what's under the surface. It takes courage to develop relationships. This vulnerability is essential to building and enjoying community with others that's meaningful, not just "spending time" together. The two are not the same.

When you're trying to do what you're learning in this chapter, you'll run into hurdles. It's awkward to ask someone how they're *really* doing (and sometimes we don't necessarily want the answer!). What if they think we're just being intrusive? Fearful of being misunderstood, you'll be tempted to make excuses in your friendships and say, "Well, it's none of my business anyway. I might inadvertently cross a boundary..."

There is a difference between what I'm describing and getting in someone's business you hardly know! That's intrusive, meddlesome, and snooping, and we all know that women (and men to a degree) can be nosy and gossipy. But your closest friends and some family members could be a different situation. Thriving in your relationships is about investing time and more attention into the unique creation God designed these important people to be and honoring that. If you do it right, it's not awkward; it's honoring.

Paying attention shows someone you love them enough to get to know them—inside and out. You accept them for who they are and celebrate that. And you are also courageous enough to point it out when you see they're going off course. In other words, you cheerlead and challenge. You must, of course, be willing to accept the same from close friends who summon the courage to challenge you when you blow it. Good friends don't take your side when you are wrong. They help you own up to your errors in a loving way. I know I can lovingly challenge a handful of friends and some family members—and they can do the same with me. If I'd had these kinds of relationships before I had an affair and divorced my husband, I would have made far different choices. Believe me. Thriving relationally with trusted girlfriends and family can keep you from doing a lot of things that mess up your life and take years, if ever, to correct.

It's important to point out that sometimes others are ignorant to the fact that they don't know how to connect or be intimate. Someone may have their boundaries up with you for some reason. In other words, what if the other person doesn't want to be known? How do we break down those walls? We can't force anyone to go deeper with us. So do we walk away? What do we say at that point?

People often confide their problems to me, and at some point in the conversation I'll usually ask, "Have you ever talked to someone in your family or friends about this struggle?" If the person attends church, I might ask if they've brought it up to their Bible study group or their pastor or elders.

You would think the people in church would feel comfortable turning to each other when life takes a turn. But more times than not, these are the first people to reply, "Oh, no. I could never tell another Christian about this..." This is a huge issue in the church and in our society as a whole. Many, many people have never shared with anyone, including their spouse (or very best friend if they're single), what is really going on in their lives. I relate. I didn't open up about my feelings for much of my life. There is so much fear of disappointing each other in a marriage, family, or close friendship. It should be safe to share our stuff with our trusted family and friends, especially after years of sharing mutual activities and hanging out together. Still, we hesitate and hold back. Some of us have years' worth of issues stuffed inside of us because we don't want to (or don't know how to) "be known" by others. And if we aren't known to others, can we really say we know anyone? Not only that, this behavior leads to negative consequences that take a heavy toll.

WHAT HAPPENS WHEN WE DON'T TALK TO OTHERS

Being known and talking about our struggles and the significant events and relationships in our lives is healthy. It's good. And it's essential to developing real relationships and authentic community. Humans are designed for community. God himself said in the first book of the Old Testament that it was not good to be all alone in the world. Like it or not, without relationships and community we cannot live the life we're designed to live. We can live without other people. But we cannot thrive.

If we keep our emotions hidden inside and bottle them up, emotional damage occurs over time. Stuffing our emotions doesn't make them go away—it makes them re-appear in ways we don't want. We can even get physically ill from the stress of repressing anger, resentment, hurt feelings, etc. Also, anyone with a propensity toward addiction can turn to mundane things like food, TV social media, busyness, and work as easily as they can abuse alcohol, pornography, and drugs as a means of relieving the pressure and stress of keeping secrets and harboring emotional wounds. Some people just want to isolate and nurse their wounds, or stay willfully ignorant of them, both of which lead to more depression. All of this negative behavior is dangerous and more common today than you would think.

The tendency is to assume everyone is too busy with their own lives to listen to our problems. We say we don't want to "burden" anyone. But is this actually just an excuse because we don't want to tell anyone our stuff? Is it fear? Is it emotional laziness? We need a new strategy. Instead, we can seek out a small community where we can be accepted. There are all kinds of communities where you would feel welcome and safe, including organizations, support groups, friend groups, sports teams, church groups, and more. You don't need a group of 30 friends to share your heart with. I have lots of friends, but there are different levels of friendship even within a larger group. There are acquaintances in life, and there are people with whom you feel more comfortable to say what's on your heart. I'm more open about my life with some people more so than others, and that circle with whom I'm intimate is pretty small. I'm not saying you must share personal details with everyone you know! Not everyone fits in the same relationship box. We have to be discerning about what we choose to share and with whom. Relationships must be developed carefully. It takes time to build a trusted community and trusted friends.

After Jeff and I remarried, our story became public. Many pastors asked us to share it with their congregations. Then we were asked to write a book. God gave us this experience to help others, and yet we had to learn to guard our hearts and not share everything with everyone. Lauren's accident was the same way. People would stop me and Lauren in the grocery store because they recognized her from the news, and we would end up talking to strangers, pouring out our hearts for 30 minutes. It was emotionally exhausting. Finally, my counselor helped me see the toll this was taking. She asked me why I felt compelled to do that with strangers. It's an encouraging story, right? Yes, but she pointed out that retelling what happened that night was needlessly re-traumatizing ourselves every time we did it. We were past the accident, but we were not over it by any means. If I ran into someone in the grocery store who asked about Lauren, I learned I could just say, "Thank you for praying for us," instead of launching into our life story.

However, I can turn to my small circle of friends and say, "Hey, this is going on with me..." I can be honest and open—

and I know they'll accept me, whatever it may be. Lately, I have had to draw on my friends during my husband's illness, especially during those times when the path ahead is not clear. When I'm worried, I talk with my husband about his illness, but I cannot talk with Jeff about all my concerns, all the time. Instead, I turn to these few trusted women in my life because I know I will not be judged. People need a sense of safety and inclusivity. Everybody wants that type of friend—and they exist out there. You just have to find one. And you have to be one.

What I'm describing is not the way 99% of people live. Cultivating relationships of every age through deeper conversation and using our words in creative ways is seriously lacking today. No wonder people feel lonely. We so seldom take the time or make the extra effort. Many people don't know why they feel lonely—even in a crowd. They experience a constant sense of low-level frustration with the quality of their lives. Women are especially apt to carry a strong sense of emptiness and lack fulfillment in the communities where they live. And they can't pinpoint the cause of their discontent. But I have a suspicion that it has a lot to do with the way true, heart-to-heart connection is rarely practiced in our culture.

FOCUSING ON OTHERS HELPS YOU

Another benefit of intentionally building community and connecting is that it makes us feel better when we do something for others. When we make ourselves emotionally available to someone (by actively listening to them, asking good follow-up questions, and being interested in their lives), they confide in us. It's funny how that works. We feel better about our own problems when we realize we're not the only ones with struggles. When you listen to someone else talk about the hardships in their lives, you have the chance to forget about all your junk for a moment.

When you take action and serve someone else, it always makes you feel better about yourself. Richness in life comes from serving. When I can love others, instead of focusing on myself and my needs, I'm much more aware of how good life can be. How many of us get caught up in our self-centeredness instead? I do. But whenever I'm selfish, I ultimately become more anxious. The more "it's all about me" I become in a desperate attempt to feel better, the worse I feel. Self-focus keeps me self-focused and doesn't make me feel better at all.

What can we do more of in our everyday routines to be there for other people? Are we paying attention to others' needs? You have to be in regular contact with people—and stay connected—in order to know what their needs are. We do that by reaching out through whatever means possible like texts, calling, visiting. People have to sense you're the kind of person they can share their needs with. You have to make time to talk to each other to know what's going on and where the real needs are. Be vulnerable. Ask the important questions. Stick your neck out. And share your heart about what's going on with you when they do the same. Of course, some relationships are one-way streets. Some people are takers; the more you give, the more they take. This is tough, and you must give thought to these types of situations.

Jeff and I have several friends who are older than us by 10 years or more. Some of them have chronic health problems, so I call and check on them. When I called a couple recently, I found out they had a real need because they had contracted Covid and had been struggling for two weeks. I offered to bring them food and leave it on their front porch. I made some soup and drove over to their house to drop it off. I could have made excuses. Their family lived nearby, and I could have assumed they were taking care of them, right? Then I wouldn't need to worry. Also, I could have said that I was too busy and besides I did not want to bother her when she was ill. I could have thought the 40-minute drive was too far, honestly. I'm guilty of this too, but I think we excuse ourselves a lot of the time from driving 40 minutes to help someone. We keep others at arm's length and just far enough away. It's not that we fail to respond to their needs because we don't care—that would be heartless. We just aren't close enough to know what these needs are! I fixed the soup and made the drive. It was not heroic. But it's the kind of things we should be doing for those we count as part of our family, circle of friends, and community.

I had a friend who lost a child many years ago. I remember how much the family and friends and her community rallied around them immediately after the child died and for many months afterward. People called and stopped by; they made food and helped them any way they could. It was all we talked about in our circle. For all their good intentions, people slowly got caught up in their own lives again. That's normal and natural. I understand that. I remember after Lauren's accident experiencing something similar. It's been years since the child died, but not for my friend who lost her daughter. The hurt is fresh, and she'll never get past that loss in her lifetime. So I make a point to remember the day my friend lost her child. It's not that difficult. I have it on my calendar to send her a quick text or call her each time that day rolls around. I just say, "I'm thinking about you today" or, "I loved your sweet girl." You wouldn't believe how meaningful that small touch is to my friend—unless you'd been through something like it. Then you'd know. You never forget those who continue to remember.

Another friend of mine is amazing because she remembers to send cards on all her friends' special days, like birthdays and anniversaries. She must have a perpetual calendar filled with all these dates. She never misses our special days—and I know she does the same with so many people in her circle and beyond. I'm so impressed by her faithfulness. Little efforts like this mean something to people. They are what weaves you into what's most important in people's lives and makes you feel more connected to those you care about.

The goal here is to encourage new growth and intentional living in every area of our lives that matters most. What you learn and put into practice hopefully elevates your level of community and catapults you to challenge yourself to take a new step forward in your understanding of and appreciation for the people God puts on your path.

PRACTICING THE LOST ARTS OF BEING HUMAN

THE LOST ART OF CONVERSATION

Examine your conversations with others. What kind of conversations do you have? Is it just fly-by-the-seat-of-your-pants talk about surface topics? Or do you regularly engage in meaningful conversation? Jeff and I know a young couple who is very intentional to meet with three or four other couples every Saturday night. They get babysitters, and they're ready for some adult conversation. The couples never talk about anything shallow. And there's no need for small talk. They've been meeting together this way for in-depth conversation for about six years, and this group is tight. How often do we spend time with people we like and have known a long time, but we never get any closer relationally?

Questions about conversation:

What does deeper conversation mean to you? Why is it important?

Deeper conversation takes being vulnerable. Would others think of you as vulnerable? Why or why not?

How do you feel when someone converses with you in a way that is deeper and more meaningful?

Here are some easy questions you can practice asking someone you want to know better:

I would love to get to know you better. Tell me three interesting things about yourself.

What are your favorite things to do? What do you consider fun?

What brings you the most joy?

As you get to know them better, you can move to deeper questions like:

What do you think are two of your gifts?

What do you struggle with?

THE LOST ART OF WRITING

I'm at the age where I don't care if I ever get another birthday or Mother's Day gift from my children. They send me the most thoughtful cards each year, and I treasure their words. When my daughters had their children, they wrote to me about how much I'd taught them about motherhood. Man. That meant so much to me. Every so often they send me a card for no reason and write something like, "Mom, I love your heart because...." and they write the most meaningful words to me. This is the good stuff and reflects the intentional effort that's largely missing in our society. But today we don't write many letters. And when we do, we don't often handwrite them.

When was the last time you sent a letter to a friend or family member about what's going on in your life or gave them a newsy update? Have you taken time to tell them how much you care about them? We can easily find ourselves writing, "This card says it all," and just signing our name and putting it in the mail. Instead, take time to do something more than sign your name under the pre-printed inscription on the card. I'm challenging you to take five or ten minutes to do a little more and open up. Put thought into what you say and concentrate on sharing emotions, not events. Catch up about all the newsy stuff, but be sure you write something meaningful also.

I also wrote letters to my parents once a week when I was in college and into my twenties. Texting and email did not exist. I just used a pad of paper or a notecard and pen. I think this is when my fetish with pens began. I still love a good pen, and I prefer to write things down on paper instead of typing. I often wrote letters to my little sister also. She recently shared with me how heartbroken she was when I left home for college. I had no idea, but those letters were so meaningful to her. Likewise, my parents kept my letters for years because they treasured them. And one of my girls told me recently that she has saved every single card and letter I have ever written to her. Wow—that brought me to tears.

Get your thoughts organized in your mind. You don't have to be a great writer to write something personal to someone. Letter writing is old-fashioned. It takes a lot of time, and you'll have to buy stamps. But this effort connects us with people in time-honored ways that tap into a tradition of communication that is older than we are. Think about what the card you select means to that person. People are insecure about their words and literally can't come up with anything, but challenge yourself. Stretch. Think of the other person. Your words can be a gift to someone. Sometimes I like the card more than the gift!

Take some time to self-evaluate. Do you regularly send greeting cards or letters to anyone? If so, think about why you do this. Consider your motives. Do you automatically send birthday, sympathy, or holiday cards and just sign "with love," followed by your name, because you have to? What do you typically write in cards—and is it heartfelt? Words have a purpose. Think about your purpose for increasing your personal touch through writing. You want deeper, thriving friendships and relationships—so it's going to take some work to get there.

Questions to ask about writing:

How much work do you have to do in this area? In other words, how can you transition from writing to fill your "obligation tank" to writing because you genuinely want to encourage and lift up someone else?

How do you feel when you receive a handwritten note that you know took thought and effort?

Who will you write this week, and what will you say?

THE LOST ART OF PHONE CALLS

Someone made the comment that we all learned who our true friends were during the pandemic. While the world isolated and turned inward, some people got really creative in the ways they connected with others in their circle since they couldn't be together in person. There were plenty of emails. And texts. And emojis. But the ones who picked up the phone and made calls (even video calls) are probably the ones who stand out in your memory as true friends.

People can stay in touch today exclusively by texting and emails—and many do. But there's something about hearing a voice on the other line that brings us closer. If we want to feel more connected and shore up a greater sense of community where we may be lacking, we'll start by thinking of new ways to reach out to the people we love. It may take us more time than just sending a text, but it will be worth it.

Questions to ask about phone calls:

Why is this practice important?

What keeps you from making phone calls to loved ones?

What is it about hearing someone's voice that is comforting? Energizing? Maybe irritating? Do you enjoy hearing others' voice? Explain.

What are your fears about making a phone call instead of texting? (For example, it will take too much time, it won't go well, we don't feel like talking and/or taking on someone else's emotions.)

Who do you know for sure will pick up whenever you call? Why?

THRIVING THE REST OF YOUR LIFE

Do you believe you can thrive? It comes down to that core belief in ourselves, doesn't it? With God's help, you can live abundantly—no matter where you've come from and regardless of what trauma you may have experienced and mistakes you have made (or will make). Your lack of confidence today is no match for the growing sense of inner peace that comes as you grow and mature into the life you were meant to live. My deepest hope is for you to continue the brave journey you've started, no matter what comes your way in the future. May you strive toward the place in your life that you believe in and dream about—that courageous, rooted, thriving place in God's plan where you address the tough stuff in life, achieve lasting change, and make a difference in the lives of those around you.

ABOUT THE AUTHOR

CHERYL SCRUGGS is the host of the Thriving Beyond Belief podcast. She loves being a wife, mom, MoMo (grandma), friend, podcast host, Biblical marriage counselor, author, and speaker. If you know Cheryl, you know you can usually find her either hanging out with her family, cooking, Pelotoning, writing, chatting, learning, or digesting God's Word! She loves to try new things, be adventurous, and love on others!

Cheryl and her husband, Jeff, are the founders of Hope Matters Marriage Ministries, A 501c3 non-profit marriage ministry offering Biblical marriage counseling to couples and individuals. Jeff and Cheryl love to share their inspiring story of finding a second chance at their marriage. They also offer online resources at www.JeffandCherylScruggs.com to help couples and individuals thrive in life and pursue God's best. Their work is based on the strong belief that when you purposefully strive to understand God's Word, you will truly live out the abundance God has for you, spiritually, emotionally, relationally, physically, and mentally.

ADDITIONAL RESOURCES

FEEL FREE TO CONTACT THE AUTHOR DIRECTLY BY visiting www.ThrivingBeyondBelief.com about having Cheryl speak at your women's event, ordering discounted bulk orders of books, and to share stories of how you're thriving right now in your life.

The Thriving Beyond Belief podcast and online community provide encouragement and support to better manage stress, create healthy relationships, and build a life to thrive beyond belief. Download your choice of episodes as Cheryl interviews insightful women and men from every walk of life about meaningful topics that challenge and inspire her audience. Stream the Thriving Beyond Belief podcast at www.ThrivingBeyondBelief.com.

Made in United States
Orlando, FL
12 December 2022